GUIMET

national museum of Asian Arts

visitor's guide

Hélène Prigent

Preface by Jean-François Jarrige
Director of Museum

Guimet musée national des ARTS ASIATIQUES

art lys

The editor thanks the curators for their careful rereading
and their judicious comments.
He also thanks the publication department of the museum
for its conscientious and efficient advice.

Certain works are sometimes missing temporarily from the rooms in order to replace them with others from the museum's reserves.
Moreover, the maps show the present-day borders for a better understanding.

Cover: View of museum

Publication Department: Denis Kilian
Graphic design: Martine Mène
PAO: Hervé Delemotte
Plans, maps: Jérôme Poitte
Editorial co-ordination: Françoise Bayle
Editorial and iconographic follow-up: Karine Barou
Production: Pierre Kegels
Iconographic documentation: Dominique Fayolle
(musée Guimet) and Caroline de Lambertye (RMN)

ISBN: 2-85495-215-4

PREFACE

The Guimet Museum, founded in 1889 by the industrialist from Lyon, Emile Guimet, was at first dedicated to the religions of Asia, Egypt and classical Antiquity. Having become afterwards the National Museum of Asian Arts, the Guimet Museum assembled collections from diverse French expeditions and scientific missions in Asia and was regularly enriched by acquisitions and important donations. During the 1920s the Guimet Museum had received the rich collections from the Indochinese Museum at Trocadero, before acquiring, in 1945, the beautiful collection of works of art from the Far East which had, until then, been conserved at the Louvre.

Following a complete renovation, finished at the beginning of 2001, the Guimet Museum was able to reorganize the presentation tours of its collections. Visitors to the museum are now able to follow the diffusion of Indian civilization and its two great religions, Hinduism and Buddhism, in Southeast Asia, and most particularly in Cambodia. Leaving from India again, they can follow the itineraries of the Silk Road towards China, Korea, and Japan, going through Afghanistan or on the Himalayan routes of Nepal and Tibet. Another tour permits one to follow the great Chinese civilization in all its historical importance and to understand its influence on Korea and Japan. However, beyond influences and contacts, the different sections of the Guimet Museum allow one to grasp the originality of the arts of the countries whose foremost works the museum has the privilege of conserving.

This new guide will be, it is hoped, a useful instrument for those who set out on a voyage offered to them by the Guimet Museum's collections.

Jean-François Jarrige
Member of the Institute

GROUND FLOOR

- Reception
- Bookstore, boutique
- India
- Southeast Asia

FIRST FLOOR

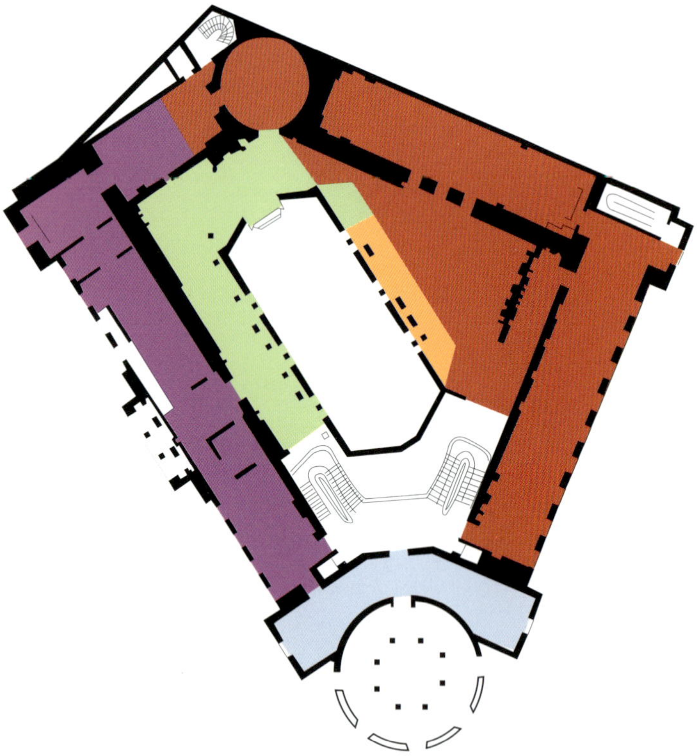

- China
- Central Asia
- Afghanistan – Pakistan
- Nepal – Tibet
- Riboud Gallery

SECOND FLOOR

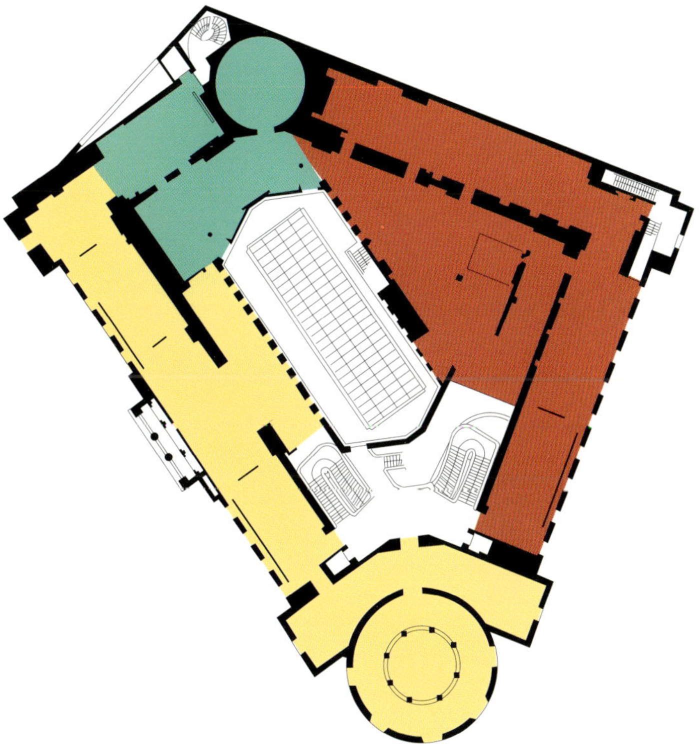

China

Korea

Japon

THIRD FLOOR
AND THE LACQUER ROTUNDA

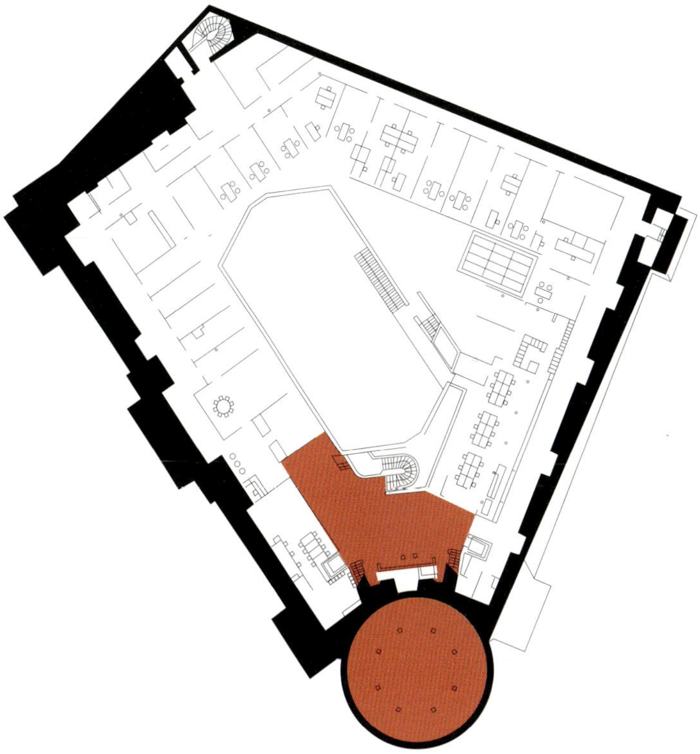

China

THE HISTORY OF AN INSTITUTION

From a Museum of Religions to the National Museum of Asian Arts-Guimet

We owe the existence of the Guimet Museum to the industrialist from Lyon, Emile Guimet (1836-1918), who was passionately interested in philosophy and ancient religions. From a scientific mission to Japan, China and India in 1876 he brought back more than three hundred paintings, six hundred statues and a few thousand Japanese and Chinese works of art. This collection was first presented at the 1878 World's Fair in Paris and was then exhibited in a new museum inaugurated in Lyon in 1879. However, Emile Guimet's ambition to increase exchanges with the international, scientific world induced him to give his collection to the French state, which committed itself to building a museum to house the collection. On November 20, 1889 the Museum of Religions opened on Place d'Iena, in Paris. As well as the Guimet collection, it assembled objects brought back from French expeditions to Tibet, Central Asia, China, and Cambodia. After the death of Emile Guimet in 1918 the museum collection was further enhanced with objects from excavations led by the French Archaeological Delegation in Afghanistan. It became a national museum in 1928 and the Khmer sculptures were transferred there after the closing of the nearby Indochinese Museum at Trocadero. The courtyard of the museum was then covered in order to shelter this extraordinary collection of Kymer art, which is the biggest in the world outside of Cambodia. Lastly, in 1945 the museum exchanged its classical and Egyptian pieces for the collections from the Asian arts department of the Louvre. Subsequently, new acquisitions and donations (the Rousset and Polain collections of Chinese terracotta, the Fournier collection of Himalayan art, the Krishna Riboud collection of Indian art...) enriched the museum considerably and made reorganization and expansion indispensable. In January 2001, after four years of work led by the architects Henri and Bruno Gaudin, the museum reopened its doors to an entirely reorganized space.

View of rooms devoted to Buddhist China, 1st floor

View of room devoted to Thailand, ground floor

View of rooms devoted to Cambodia, ground floor

INDIA

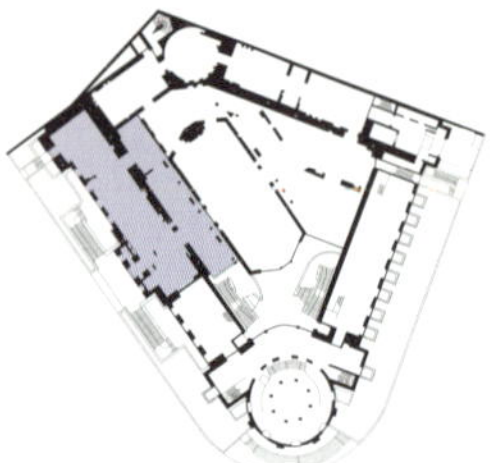

These works
are situated
on the ground floor

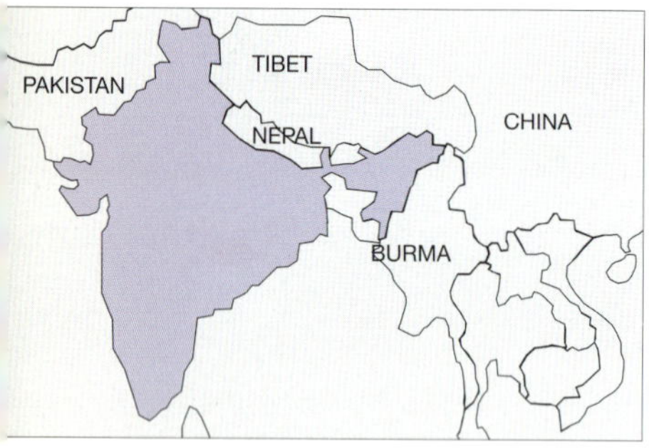

Buddhist art

We know very little of the prehistory of the Indian subcontinent: excavations revealed a first settlement in the northwest of the peninsula in the seventh millennium BC and then a culture already evolved in the south of Afghanistan from the fourth to the first millennium.

From the third millennium, a prosperous urban civilization sea-trading with Mesopotamia lived in the Valley of the Indus until the Aryan invasion. We know the seals, the red earthenware and the black drawings from the sites of Mohenjo-Daro and Harrappa.

It wasn't until the coming of Buddhism to India that the first great religious art of the country was born. Sculpture played a major role here, around the *stupa*, a fundamental Buddhist monument which is a sort of dome-shaped grave mound, or tumuli, surrounded by a balustrade. Buddhists honor it with offerings. Between the 1st and 4th century two artistic centres produced the main part of the sculptures of India. In the North, the school of Mathura, the capital of the Kusana Empire, heralded already the role the body would play. In the southeast, the centre of Amaravati excelled in narrative bas-reliefs like *The Assault of Mara*, where the presence of Buddha is suggested only by his empty throne. It was only towards the end of the 1st century that he was represented, characterized by the protuberance in the top of the head, the tuft of hair between the eyes, the elongated earlobes and the presence of wheels in the palms of the hand.

Buddhist art reached its peak under the Gupta Empire (6th century). The principal works of the period came from the workshops of Mathura and Sarnath. A perfect balance of forms and delicate execution were in harmony with the serenity of Buddha: a subtly shaped figure is thus observed in a draped garment, which only suggested the belt which it covered. Buddhism was supplanted by Hinduism and disappeared from the Indian peninsula at the beginning of the 13th century.

The Assault of Mara, stupa casing slab, southern India, Andhra Pradesh, Gantasala, Amaravati School, 2nd century, "marble" limestone, 177 x 94 cm

Nagaraja, serpent king, northern India, Uttar Pradesh, Mathura region, Kusana period, 2nd century, red sandstone, 116 x 66 cm

Buddha, northern India, Uttar Pradesh, Mathura region, Gupta period, 1st half or mid 5th century, pink sandstone, 142 x 54 cm

Buddhism and Hinduism

In the second half of the second millennium BC the Aryans, shepherds who came from Persia and Northern India, settled in the Ganges valley and spread the spiritual traditions of four sacred texts, the *Veda*, as well as their language, Sanskrit, which would remain the religious and scholarly language of Northern India until modern times. The most ancient religion practiced in India, Brahmanism, stems directly from the *Veda*. Based on the belief in the cycles of reincarnation, it was enriched with the writing of two types of texts, the *Brahmana*, which comments on the *Veda*, and the *Upanisad*, which is of a more esoteric nature, written between the 6th and 3rd century BC. It integrates the legends of the two great Indian epics, the *Ramayana* and the *Mahabharata*.
In the 6th century BC Buddhism appeared. Taking up once more the belief in the cycles of rebirth, it offers, through the person of Buddha (The Enlightened One), whose historical presence under the name of Sakyamuni is situated between 556 and 476 BC, a model of wisdom based on the renouncement of desire. Adopted by a sovereign of the Maurya dynasty in the 3rd century BC, Buddhism, from that moment, coexisted peacefully with Brahmanism.
A new form of the ancient Brahmanism, Hinduism, which appeared towards the 2nd century BC, distinguished itself through the role of two principal divinities, Shiva and Vishnu. Brahma, the creator of the universe had only secondary role in the religion whereas Vishnu assumed the continuity of the universe and Shiva was the creative force. This triad dominated many pantheons.

Head of Buddha, Gupta period, ca. 430-435, northern India, Uttar Pradesh, Mathura, pink sandstone, 50 x 30 cm

INDIA

These works
are situated
on the ground floor

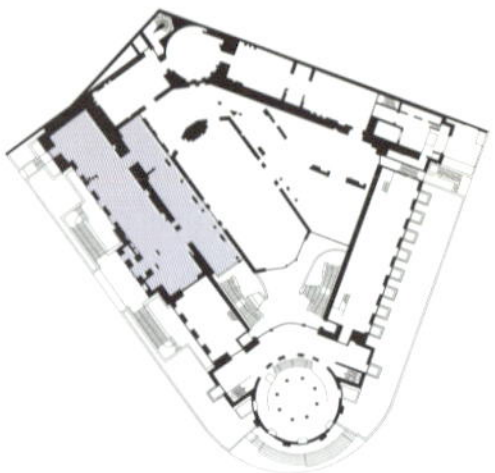

Hindu art

Appearing in the 1st and 2nd centuries, Hindu art eventually replaced Buddhist art. Stylistically the two arts first of all originated in a common aesthetic and at the end of the 7th century one still saw the canons of the Gupta style in the treatment of the eyes and the arch of the eyebrows of the figure of the monumental *Ekamukhalinga*. The phallic symbol of Shiva, meant to evoke his creative force, the *linga*, represented by a more or less sculpted oblong form, was given the most important place in the sanctuaries consecrated to God. Hindu art however soon distinguished itself with a fuller composition and richly adorned figures, like the *Vishnu* of the Hoysala period. Each of these iconographic elements was strictly codified, from the measurements and attributes of the deities to the expressions on their faces. In the same way that one sought, in depicting such-and-such a deity, to gain his favors, one scrupulously respected the iconographic indications given by the texts, for fear of seeing the deity transformed into a harmful force. This is because, and it's another characteristic of Hinduism, all the deities possess several aspects, alternately beneficial and harmful, like the cosmic forces they incarnate. Thus it is for Shiva "the king of dance", represented with remarkable skill by the bronze makers of the Chola period (11th century). In a circle of flames, the deity with four arms does the cosmic dance which at the same time, destroys and recreates the worlds, while he crushes the demon incarnating ignorance and evil with his right foot. Conserved in a temple devoted to Shiva, this sculpture was carried in procession during certain religious feasts. To the scale and simplicity of Buddhist art was thus substituted the dynamism of Hindu art. This wouldn't be called into question by the Moslem conquest of the 12th century.

Ekamukhalinga, northeast India, Bihar, Gaya region, pre-Pala period, late 7th or early 8th century, black chlorite, H: 70 cm

Vishnu Vasudeva, southern India, Karnataka, Hoysala period, 12th century, chlorite schist, 105 x 47 cm

Right page:
Shiva Nataraja, Lord of the dance, southern India, Tamil Nadu, Chola period, 11th century, bronze, 96 x 80 cm

These works are situated on the ground floor

The feminine deities

In the sanctuaries of India, the multiple representations of nude, sensuous feminine deities can surprise the Western visitor. They correspond to a conception characteristic of the Buddhist and Hindu religions for which the body, far from being linked to the idea of sinning, participates in the cycle of regeneration.

The iconographic model of feminine deities doesn't vary whether it is integrated into a Buddhist or Hindu edifice: full but graceful forms, ample bosom, weight on one hip accentuated by a slender waist, and the deep-set navel. In the temples, these sculptures are placed on door jambs when they are river deities symbolizing the Ganges and its affluent, or on the walls for mothers or tree deities. Linked to nature in which they exalt the living forces of exuberance and fertility, they possess, like nature, a fertile power. Thus the tree deities were known to be capable of making a tree flower simply by their presence nearby.

Compared to these beneficial powers, heirs to ancient religions celebrating nature, there were other deities, the *matrika* or "mothers" which incarnated harmful or destructive forces, natural calamities and epidemics in particular. Integrated into the Hindu pantheon, they became the *sakti*, that is to say the feminine energy associated with certain gods from whom they acquired attributes. However, they especially joined in the multiple manifestations of the Great Hindu Goddess, the incarnation of cosmic energy, whose religion spread during the first millennium. Like Kali, one of the wives of Shiva, they evoke terrible aspects. They are often represented with bulging eyes, hair standing on end and curled up lips baring her teeth.

Matrika, southern India, Tamil Nadu, early Chola period, late 9th-early 10th century, granite, 115 x 67 cm

Tree deity, Madhya Pradesh or Rajasthan, 10th-11th century, sandstone, 78 x 38 cm

Feminine deity,
Rajasthan, Harshagiri (Sikar),
Purana Mahadeva temple,
ca. 973, sandstone, 73 x 32 cm

SOUTH EAST ASIA

These works
are situated
on the ground floor

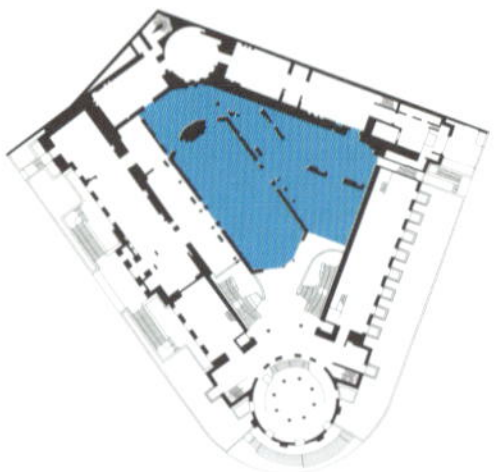

CAMBODIA

The pre-Angkorian period (1st-8th century)

The first Cambodian kingdom is attested between the 1st and 7th century. From this maritime empire, which appears to have dominated the south of present-day Cambodia and the Mekong Delta, there remain objects from the Mediterranean world, Iran, India and China. The last rulers of this kingdom had Sanskrit names which attest to the Indianization of the country. Khmer mythology confirms this influence: the dynasty was born through the union of a princess snake (the snake or *naga* is an emblem of Cambodia, a country of water) with a Brahmin. From the middle of the 6th century Cambodia appeared divided into several kingdoms. The first remains of Cambodian statuary date from this period. Stemming directly from Indian culture, they attest to the coexistence, in Khmer country, of the two principal religions of India. Thus, for Hinduism, a great Harihara, combining the dual qualities of Vishnu (Hari) and of Shiva (Hara), took up the Indian model: the left half of the statue wears the tiara of Vishnu, his emblematic disc and his draped clothing, whereas on the right one finds a cresent-shaped chignon, as well as the third eye, tiger-skin clothing and the trident, the emblem of Shiva. As often with pre-Angkorian sculpture, the statue possesses a supporting arc ensuring its stability. As for Buddhism, it is represented by several *bodhisattva*, beings "promised Enlightenment" who, in compassion for beings, delay this Enlightenment. In the lengthening of the torso of the *bodhisattva* from the 8th century, as in the stylization and idealization of the body of the goddess of the same period, one recognizes the emergence of varying local characteristics. If this diversity undoubtedly reflected a split in power – there were several royal lineages in the country in the 8th century – it also revealed a liberation from Indian art, which is apparent in the hieratic quality of the figures.

Harihara, Cambodia, Asram Maha Rusei, Prei Krabas district, Takeo province, Phnom Da style, 7th century (?), sandstone, 174 x 60 cm

Bodhisattva Lokesvara, Thailand, Prakon Chai (?), Buriram province, 8th century, bronze, 64 x 28 cm

Feminine deity, Cambodia, Koh Krieng, Sambor district, Kratie province, Prei Khmeng style, 8th century, sandstone, 135 x 52 cm

SOUTH EAST ASIA

These works
are situated
on the ground floor

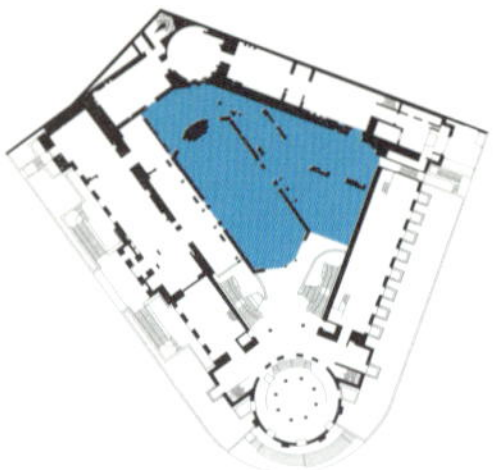

CAMBODIA

From the foundation of Angkor to Angkor Vat (9th-11th century)

Feminine deity, Cambodia, Preah Vihear, Preah Vihear district and province, Baphuon style, 11th century, sandstone

Towards 790 a name appeared in Cambodia that would leave its mark on the history of the country: Jayavarman II. After liberating his people from the domination of, in all likelihood, an Indonesian invader, this king had himself crowned "universal sovereign" in 802 and created a centralized State capable of controlling the waters from the Great Lake whose yearly floods ravaged the centre of the country.

Towards 900, Angkor became the capital of the kingdom: the first temple, composed of five terraces and one hundred and nine sanctuary-towers called the Bakheng was erected there. It was dedicated to Shiva who, more than the other gods, was associated with royal power. A head of this god is characteristic of the first Angkorian art: the extreme stylization of the features is probably explained by the influence exerted by the statuary in metal. This stylization was even more accentuated when Jayavarman IV usurped power and in 928 chose a new capital in Koh Ker.

In 944 the monarchy came back to Angkor and the city developed remarkably. A new temple dedicated to Shiva was built there, Banteay Srei, from where comes the pediment narrating an episode from the *Mahabharata*, the battle of Sunda and Upasunda: the gods, worried about the power of these two demons, sent them to the nymph Tilottama. Led astray by love, they armed themselves with tremendous clubs and killed each other. This work reflects the delicate style of the art of Banteay Srei, which lasted until the beginning of the 11th century.

In 1002 a new dynasty took power and erected a number of monuments in Angkor; the most famous is the temple of Baphuon. The sculpted feminine divinity in sandstone evokes this style combining simplicity and gentleness: the modeling of the bosom and the skirt which goes up on the hips exposing the navel reveal a subtle knowledge of the harmony of the forms. Henceforth Khmer art achieved remarkable skills that the great temple Visnuite of Angkor Vat, constructed in the first half of the 12th century, illustrates the culmination.

Shiva, Cambodia, Phnom Bok, Banteay Srei district, Siem Reap province, Bakheng style, late 9th-early 10th century, sandstone, H: 46 cm

Pediment, Cambodia, Banteay Srei, Banteay Srei district, Siem Reap province, west porch *gopura* east III, Banteay Srei style, ca. 967, sandstone, 195 x 269 cm

SOUTH EAST ASIA

These works
are situated
on the ground floor

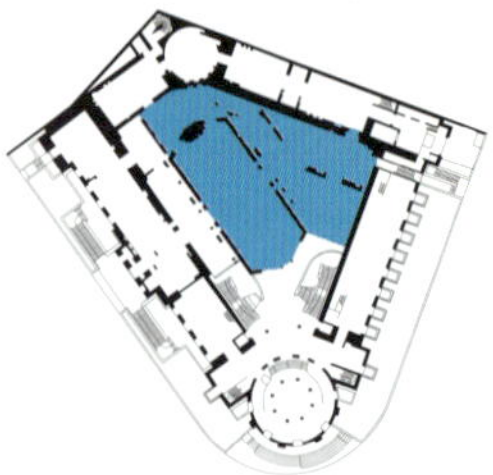

CAMBODIA

The apotheosis and the end of Angkor (12th-15th century)

In 1177 the city of Angkor was sacked by the armies of a neighboring kingdom, Champa. Jayavarman VII drove the invaders back before having himself crowned king in 1181 and extending his kingdom all over continental Southeast Asia. The legend tells that he constructed more than all of his predecessors put together. Many Kymer monuments date in fact from his reign; the most well-known is the city of Angkor Thom with its "tower of faces" and, in its centre, the temple of Bayon, which gave its name to the style of the period. From this temple comes the group of nine dancers which displays an astonishing imagination and an accomplished art of composition.

The Bayon is a Buddhist temple like all the sanctuaries constructed under the reign of Jayavarman VII. The king actually raised a complex form of Buddhism, Mahayana, to the rank of official religion and sculptors endeavoured from that time on to represent the Buddha in the contemplation which followed his Enlightenment. The smile of Angkor was born, expressing both compassion and determination at the same time. It is found on the lips of a sculpted head of Jayavarman VII, suggesting an affinity between the Sage and the pious king who was said to suffer more from the pain of his subjects than they themselves did. Jayavarman VII would thus be the only Khmer king whose effigy would be conserved; it happens too though that one recognizes the queen Jayarajadevi, the first wife of the sovereign, in the statue of the goddess Tara. After the death of Jayavarman VII in 1219, there were no more great building sites in Angkor. In the 14th century, the Khmer adopted Theravada Buddhism, originating from Ceylan, which is still the religion of the Cambodians today; the statuary took on the characteristics of humility and reserve. In 1431 the monarchy abandoned the capital, beset by the expansionist aims of the Thais. Angkor would be the capital for the last time in the 16th century, before being overrun by vegetation under which the Westerners would discover it three centuries later.

Head, presumed portrait of Jayavarman VII, Cambodia, Angkor region (?), Bayon style, late 12th-early 13th century, sandstone, 41 x 25 cm

Prajnaparamita or Tara (?), presumed portrait of Jayarajadevi, Cambodia, Preah Khan, Angkor, Siem Reap district and province, Bayon style, late 12th-early 13th century, sandstone, 124 x 50 cm

Pediment frieze, detail, Cambodia, Bayon (Angkor Thom), Siem Reap district and province, Bayon style, late 12th-early 13th century, sandstone, 60 x 276 cm

Right page: *The giants' causeway*, Cambodia, Preah Khan, Angkor, district and province of Siem Reap, Bayon style, late 12th-early 13th century, sandstone

SOUTH EAST ASIA

These works are situated on the ground floor

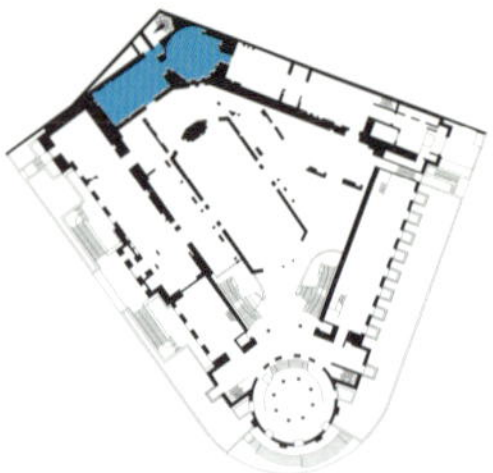

THE KINGDOM OF CHAMPA AND VIETNAM

Although the existence of the kingdom of Champa, along the eastern coast of Vietnam, is attested to the 2nd century AD, it wasn't until the 7th century that sculptures representative of Cham art were found. Discoveries on the site of Mi Son, in the north of Champa, where a temple dedicated to Shiva had been erected, attested to the assimilation of Indian culture, while the aspect of the faces and the bodies revealed the persistence of local traditions. From the enthronement of Indravarman I, in 875, a basically Buddhist art developed, most of whose remains come from an immense monastery built by the king in Dong Duong. A door keeper, who was perhaps part of these remains and whose threatening aspect betrays a Chinese influence, displays the characteristics of the sculpture of the period: flat noses, bulging eyes, and the luxuriance of the decorative motifs. At the end of the reign of Indravarman I, towards 910, the styles of Tra Kieu and of Mi Son marked the return of a more sober art. From the 11th century the kingdom of Champa, threatened by Vietnam, withdrew towards the south. It was there that the last great style was born in Binh Dinh, where several sanctuary-towers, each one having the name of a precious material, were built between the 11th and 13th century. From the Silver Tower comes a great Shiva with stylized forms recognizable in the frontal third eye and the cresent of the moon on her hair. In 1471 Champa was conquered by Vietnam for good.

As for Vietnam, the culture called Dong Son developed in the north, during the second half of the first millennium BC; the art of bronze was very developed there, as a large ritual drum displays. However from 111 BC until 905 AD Vietnam was under Chinese domination and all its arts, ceramics in particular, were strongly influenced by Chinese culture. This influence remained a determining factor after the country's attainment of independence.

Ritual drum, Vietnam, Song Da basin, Dong Son II culture, middle of 1st millennium BC, bronze, H: 61 cm; D: 78 cm

Temple guardian Dvarapala, Vietnam, Dong Duong, Quang Nam province, Dong Duong style, last quarter 9th-early 10th century, sandstone, H: 66 cm

Shiva, Vietnam, Thap Banh it (Silver Tower), Binh Dinh province, transition between Mi Son and Thap Mam styles, 11th-12th century, sandstone, traces of later polychromy, 150 x 105 cm

SOUTH EAST ASIA

These works are situated on the ground floor

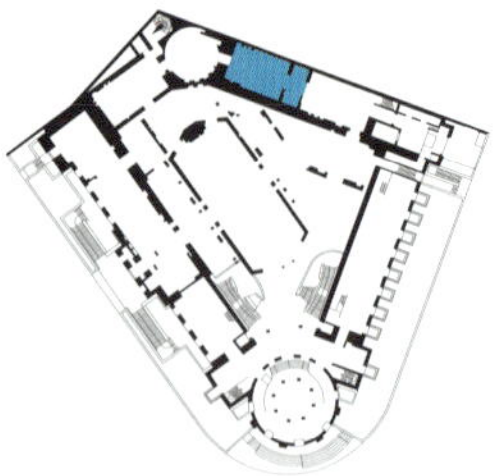

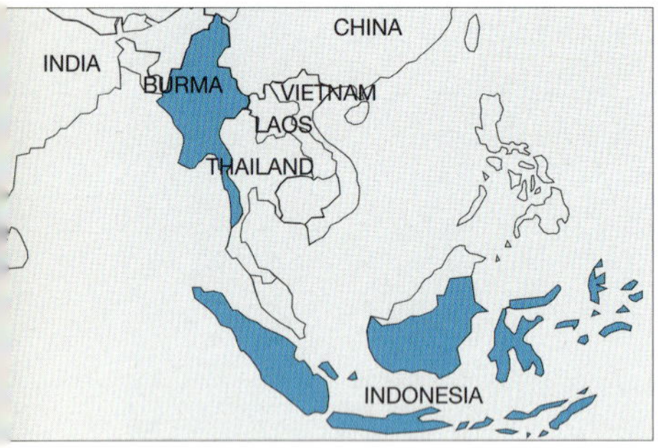

INDONESIA AND BURMA

From the first centuries AD, several Indianized kingdoms were shown to be in Indonesia; their prosperity was ensured by the maritime routes connecting India and China to Southeast Asia. From the centre of Java, where, during the 8th century, the temple of Borobudur was erected, came the most beautiful works of the island. Illustrating a Hindu or Buddhist iconography, according to the confession of succeeding kings to the throne they reveal, in the delicacy and grace of the sculptures, an Indian influence which is manifest for example in the bronze statuette representing Avalokitesvara. From the 10th century, at the moment when the kingdoms set up in the eastern part of the island, Indonesian art became more embellished, with adornment taking a dominant place. This art disappeared at the dawn of the 16th century when Islam established itself in Java. Bali was the last center where Indian traditions remained alive.

As in Indonesia, the first populations to settle on the territory of Burma, the Puy and the Mon, and their kingdoms, were Indianized in the first centuries AD. With the accession of the Burmese kingdom of Pagan in the 9th century, the country was unified and its capital, Pagan, became one of the most brilliant cities of Southeast Asia. If the art which developed there kept traces of earlier local cultures, it was especially influenced by the Indian statuary from Bengal and Bihar, and developed Buddhist iconography with sobriety. Adorning the niches in the walls of the sanctuaries, great statues of Buddha were made to be seen from the front, as the statue in wood representing an adorned Buddha. In the 14th century the kingdom was divided up and it wasn't until the 16th century that the Burmese dynasty of Toungoo reunited the country, but the art then had evolved towards an overabundance of decoration and only a few regions – in the north of the country where the Shan dominated and the Arakan to the west – conserved the original characteristics.

Bodhisattva Avalokitesvara, Indonesia, Java, art of central Java, 8th-9th century, bronze, 35 x 20 cm

Crowned Buddha, Burma, Myanmar, post-Pagan Burmese art, 14th century, gilt-lacquered wood, 187 x 50 cm

SOUTH EAST ASIA

These works
are situated
on the ground floor

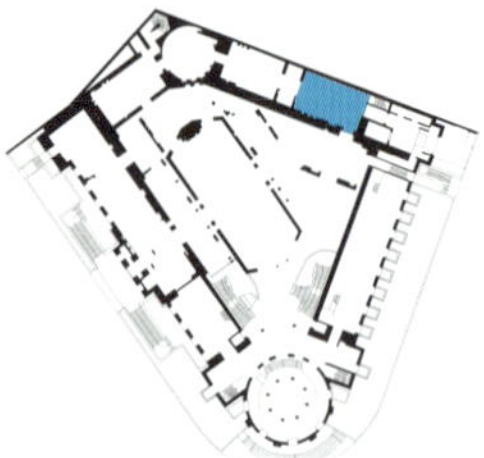

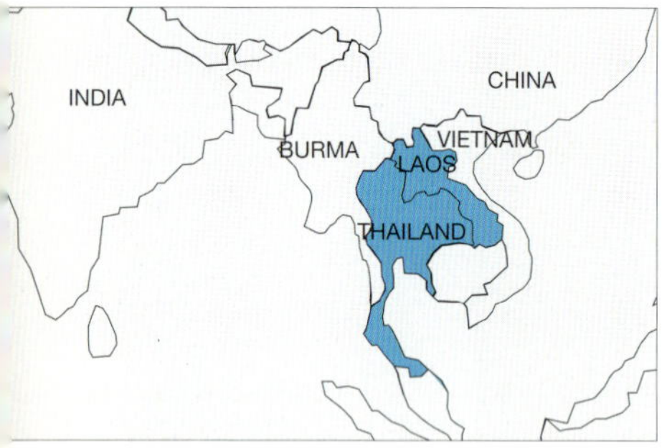

THAILAND AND LAOS

Situated in the heart of Southeast Asia, between the worlds influenced by China and India, Thailand was influenced by Indian culture at the beginning of the first millennium AD and adopted its language and its religions. The art which developed there was principally inspired by Buddhism but showed a great diversity and very pronounced local traits, reflecting the mosaic of peoples settled on its territory: Khmer, Indonesian, and Mon. It was just after the foundation of the kingdom of Ayutthaya, in the 13th century that these local particularities tended to fade away but not entirely disappear. Several schools then came into being in the successive capitals of the kingdom: the school of Sukhothai, from the end of the 8th to the 15th century, whose graphic developments exerted a considerable influence; the school of Lanna which, from the 13th century, gathered traditions from the northern regions; the school of Ayutthaya which, from the 14th to the 18th century, combined the contribution of the school of Sukhothai with Khmer elements; and lastly the school of Bangkok which, from the end of the 18th century, preserved the traditions of the art of Ayutthaya. The distinctive characteristics of each school were all the more apparent as their artists always used the same iconographic themes inspired by Buddhism; eloquent in this respect is the confrontation of two Buddhas belonging respectively to the schools of Lanna and Ayutthaya.

At first primarily dependent on Khmer culture, the art of Laos later assimilated contributions from Burma and Thailand. Unfortunately, evidence of this art before the 16th century is rare and the majority of the works conserved date from the 18th and 19th centuries. The influence of Buddhism in Laos, as in Thailand, was predominant.

Wheel of the Law, Thailand, Mon art of Dvaravati,
8th or 9th century, sandstone, D: 160 cm

Head of Buddha, Thailand, Ayutthaya art, 14th century, bronze, H: 28 cm

Head of Buddha, Thailand, art of Lanna, 15th century, bronze, H: 22 cm

CHINA

These works
are situated
on the 1st floor

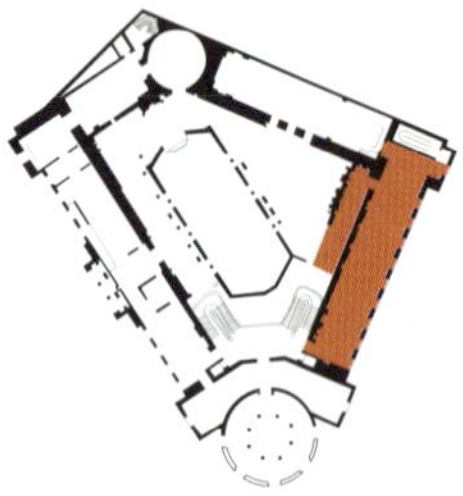

ANCIENT CHINA

From the Neolithic to the Iron Age

China is one of the oldest human settlements: the first traces of the Hominidae go back to a million years ago, the first vestiges of civilization date from the tenth millennium, and pottery and the beginning of agriculture are attributed to the seventh millennium BC. In the fourth and third millennium, three great cultures were outstanding. In the north, the culture of Yangshao, called "painted pottery" spread over the central plain where it produced handcrafted pottery decorated with black designs. More to the east the culture of Hongshan developed; it worked with jade and produced high-pedestalled tripod pottery. Lastly, in the low Yangtze region, the culture of Liangzhu displayed the use of jade and bone.

Bronze appeared under the Shang, the first Chinese dynasty, in the 16th century BC, the same time that the first palaces were built and handwriting was invented. The forms and decorations of the vases in bronze, casted in section-moulds, varied in function with their use in offering rituals. The overthrow of the Shang by the western Zhou in 1077 brought no big change and the art of bronze continued to prosper, yielding casted pieces of a remarkable delicacy. Bronze was sometimes worked according to the lost-wax casting process from the Spring and Autumn period, which marked, in 770 BC, the weakening of Zhou's power. Three centuries later, several rival states, combating kingdoms, shared the territory while in the footsteps of Confucius and Laozi (Lao Tsu) emerged a group of men of letters, the *Shi.* During the same period the sacrificing of humans started to disappear: henceforth one began to substitute servants, who were until then buried next to the dead, with figurines called *mingqi.*

In 246, an ambitious prince, Zheng, ascended to the throne and annexed all the states in ten years, "like the caterpillar devours the blackberry bush leaf", wrote the historian Sima Qian in the 1st century BC. The first Chinese Empire was born.

Standing figure, central China,
ancient kingdom of Chu,
Warring Kingdoms period,
5th century BC, wood,
traces of lacquer and polychromy,
human hair, silk fragments, H: 53.5 cm

Piece of harnass, mask, China,
Western Zhou Dynasty,
11th-8th century BC, H: 23 cm

Long-necked bottle, northwest China, Gansu, Majiayao culture,
ca. 2700 BC, buff-coloured terracotta, brown-painted decoration, 22.3 x 17.8 cm

These works are situated on the 1st floor

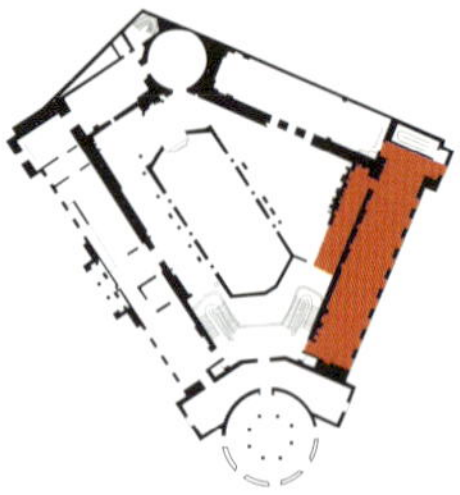

ANCIENT CHINA

The foundation of the Empire

When he founded the Empire in 221 BC, Zheng had the ambition to restore the political unity of the ancient Zhou dynasty. He launched a military campaign to the limits of the Empire, built the Great Wall along the borders and diminished *Shi* authority by burning all the classics in 213. His glory is especially due however to his mausoleum, whose existence, attested to by the historian Sima Qian, was confirmed by excavations: "At beginning of his reign, he planned and had Mount Li dug. Then [...] he mobilized 70,000 workers, having undergone the torture of castration, to do the work. The earth was dug until water was reached and bronze was poured for the exterior cover of the sarcophagus. [...] A map was made of the Empire, the one hundred rivers and the vast sea were traced with mercury and machinery put it in movement. Celestial bodies were represented on the ceiling. Lamps that could burn for a very long time were made from seal fat." With its infantry of 6,000, its horses and its grooms, its monks, and its workers the grandiose mausoleum became a model for Chinese lords and the funeral statuary was a foremost art as the head of a soldier illustrates.

The statuary of the Han, also made with great delicacy, was innovative in representing characters which until then had been ignored by sculptors: servants, musicians, cooks...with faces full of alacrity. The Han, while managing the imperial administration when it ascended to power in 206 BC, restored honour to literature, to Confucianist doctrine and to a more humanist art. Even the horse, until then exclusively associated with the world of war, became a symbol of social prestige. The dynasty collapsed in 220 AD. One had to wait for the Northern Wei, of nomad origin, who ascended to power in 386, to see the country partly reunified. In contact with Gandhara, the art of this period achieved a remarkable grace and suppleness.

Head of a soldier, northern China, Qin dynasty, 3rd century BC, gray terracotta, H: 11 cm

Head of a horse, central China, Sichuan, late Han Dynasty, 1st-3rd century, gray terracotta, H: 36 cm

Musician, northern China, Wei dynasty, 1st half of 6th century, molded terracotta and traces of polychromy on slip, 16 x 10.1 cm

Standing man, northern China, Shaanxi, early Han dynasty, 2nd century BC, gray terracotta, red slip, H: 60 cm

CHINA

These works are situated on the 1st floor

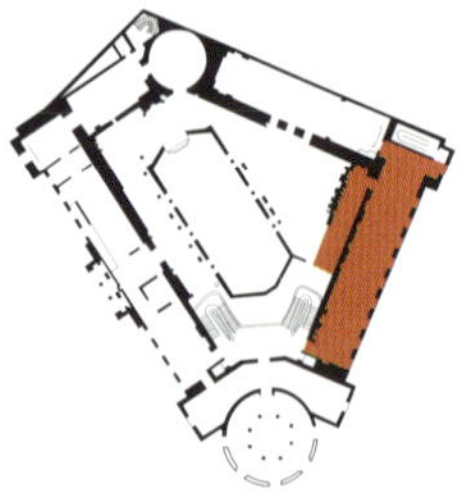

ANCIENT CHINA

The height of the first Empire: the Tang

If the unification of northern and southern China and the development of communication routes between the two was the work of the Sui, it was with their successors, the Tang, that the Empire was truly unified. Supported by an unprecedented economic expansion and nourished by a vast network of exchanges linked to the increasing influence of China, Central Asia, Korea and Vietnam, commerce was remarkably prosperous at that time. Like the capital of the Empire, Chang'an, the most important in Asia, cities located on the main routes became cosmopolitan centers where wealth is exchanged, but also ideas, cultures and customs. From the Persia of the Sassanides, whose last sovereign found refuge in the Chinese court, the Tang borrowed polo, played equally by men and women. Supple funerary figures depicted playing, leaning on their horse's neck, also showed the influence of India, whose statuary were at that time largely spread over Central Asia. Closer attention paid to the movement of the body as well as to a greater realism was henceforth the orientation of Chinese sculpture, all the while conserving its traditional characteristics of simplicity and restraint. This alliance produced an art of a rare elegance which, in the discreet twist of the shoulders of a court lady, the leaning bodies of two musicians or the gracious play of the arms of a dancer, brilliantly associates sensuality and seriousness, movement and interiority, and refinement and vigour. In the 8th century, this court art, encouraged by the generosity of a prosperous society, was so successful that funerals had to be regulated by limiting the number of *Mingqi* and forbidding precious materials to be used to make them. The rebellion led by the border general An Lushan from 755 tolled the end of this sumptuous art. The Tang Dynasty collapsed at the dawn of the 10th century.

Polo player, northern China, Tang dynasty, 1st half of 8th century, red terracotta, slip, polychromy, H: 31 cm

Pair of dancers, northern China, Tang dynasty, mid 7th century, white terracotta, lead glaze, H: 17 cm

Right page: *Court lady*, northern China, Tang dynasty, late 7th-early 8th century, terracotta with slip and paint, 38.7 x 11.5 cm

CHINA

These works
are situated
on the 1st floor

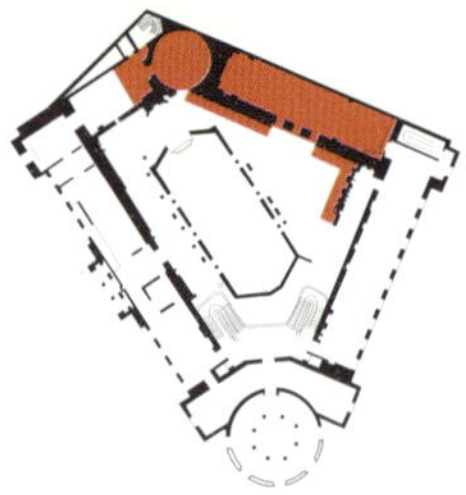

BUDDHIST CHINA

Introduced in China from the middle of the 1st century by missionaries and traders who followed a series of trade routes, the Silk Roads, Buddhism actively developed during the periods which preceded the foundation of the Tang Empire, thanks to the support of the barbarian dynasties. The first artistic centre of Chinese Buddhism was in the 4th century in Dunhuang, the seat of a commander's residence and the meeting point of two silk trade routes. The influence of the art of Gandhara was appreciable here.
Then came the great rock sanctuaries founded upon the initiative of the Northern Wei, in Yungang first and then, from 494, in Longmen, from where came the fragment of a relief depicting a bodhisattva royally relaxed. The angular rendering of Greek-Buddhist draping and the lengthening of bodies, such as appeared in Longmen, are characteristic of the evolution of Chinese Buddhist art from Gandhara. In the middle of the 6th century however there was a reaction against what was becoming conventional art. It resulted in, under the Tang Dynasty, a fuller and more realistic sculpture. Whether it's the slender body of a celestial dancer or the stocky silhouette of a protector of the Orient, bodies are fully present and faces are more expressive. In the 8th century, Buddhism was completely integrated into Chinese religious practices, with the Confucianism of men of letters and the Taoism of the nobility. An important work of translation was undertaken, helped by the pilgrimages of monks who came to India to bring copies of ancient, sacred texts. More and more prosperous, all the more so because they didn't pay taxes, Buddhists monasteries eventually worried the authorities. A persecution was started in 843 and ended two years later with the banning of Buddhism. All the same it remained an important spiritual force. After the fall of the Tang, it remained in the north of the country, but the arts it inspired generally declined.

Monk carrying books,
central Asia, Dunhuang,
9th century, paint, ink, gold,
and colours on silk, 79 x 52 cm

Celestial king (lokapala), central Asia, Dunhuang, Magao caves (Gansu), Tang Dynasty, 8th century, polychrome wood with traces of gilt, 99 x 47.5 cm

Bodhisattva sitting in royal relaxation, northern China, Longmen caves (Henan), Six Dynasties period (222-589), early 6th century, limestone, H: 41 cm

CENTRAL ASIA

These works are situated on the 1st floor

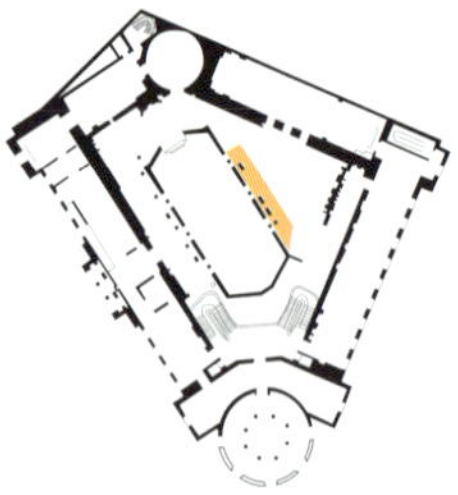

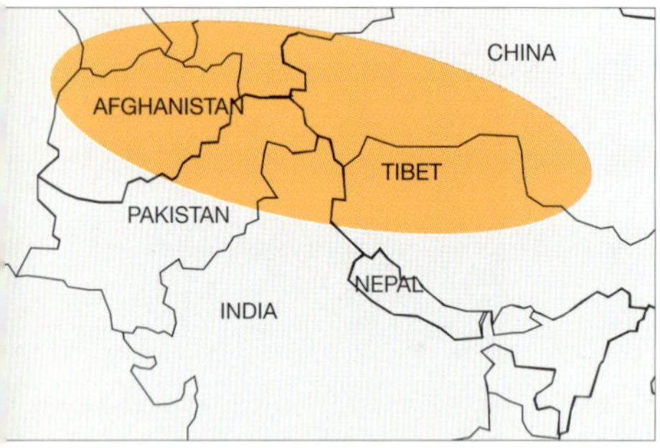

BETWEEN CHINA AND INDIA: SERINDIA

Serindia was a name invented in the 1920's by an English archeologist, Aurel Stein, to designate the immense region lying between China and India, and which covers the eastern Silk Roads. Touched by Buddhism in the 2nd century, Serindia developed a brilliant and unique civilization for a thousand years, sustained by trade routes which, coming from Antioche, Alexandria and Byzance, joined the two ends, the Mediterranean Sea and the Middle Empire. The missionaries, monks and traders moved along the routes peacefully, assuring the wealth of the land.

In this region principally made up of small, independent kingdoms a syncretic art developed. This is because Serindia assimilated many artistic movements: Gandhara art, Indian art, the culture of the Indo-Greek kingdoms like Bactrian, and lastly, the Chinese art of the Sui and the Tang. The *bodhisattva* and the feminine deities, with slightly chubby faces enlivened with a serene and cheerful smile, wore extravagant hairstyles topped with laurels and tiaras. The narrative compositions were original too: formed by an assembly of figures moulded in dry or baked clay they displayed a mastery of the art. As for the harmony of proportions, the symmetry of the scenes and the idealization of the figures, they irresistibly evoked Greek antique perfection.

From the second half of the 8th century several political upheavals struck the different empires – the progression of Islam towards the West, the rebellion of An Lushan and the decline of the Tang in China and then the expansion of the Tibetan kingdom in Central Asia – hurt the commercial network. Cut off from the Chinese Empire, sometimes even from one another, the oasis still survived for a few more centuries before being abandoned and disappearing under the sand. The sanctuaries and monasteries of Serindia would be rediscovered by archaologists at the end of the 19th century who were then able to trace the progression of Buddhist art all along the Silk Roads until China.

Heroic acts of the bodhisattva, detail,
Tumshuq (Xinjiang), Toqquz-sarai, large temple B,
6th-early 7th century, dried clay, 75 x 76 cm

Head crowned with feathered tiara, Tumshuq (Xinjiang), Toqquz-sarai, small temple D, 6th-early 7th century, dried clay partially baked, 24 x 11 cm

PAKISTAN AFGHANISTAN

These works are situated on the 1st floor

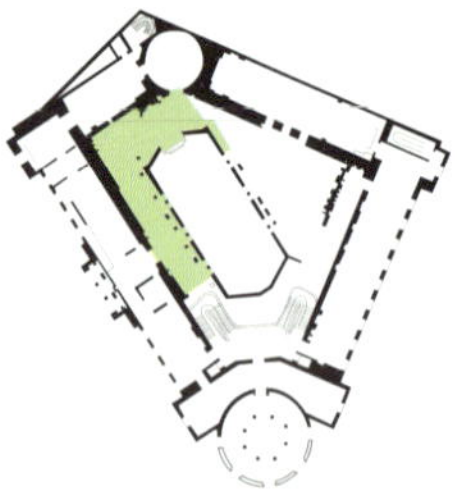

The art of Gandhara

Like that of Serindia, the history of the regions which today cover a big part of Afghanistan and Pakistan owe a lot to their geographical position: located in the heart of Asia they were crossed by trade routes which connected the Mediterranean Sea, India and China. From the third millennium BC, the Mundigak civilization in Afghanistan, which reached its peak around 2500, exchanged with Mesopotamia, Suse and the valley of the Indus; at the end of the millennium, Bactrian developed similar exchanges.

Around 1700 BC these exchanges stopped. They resumed in the 6th century with the conquest of Afghanistan by Cyrus the Great, who integrated it into the Persian dynasty of Achaemenids until the conquest of Alexander the Great. When he died in 323 the South was conquered by the Indian dynasty of Maurya, which introduced Buddhism there around the 3rd century BC. The Scythes and the Parthians in turn invaded the country. It was however the Tocharians, nomads from the north of China, who annexed it in the 1st century AD. Through the relations they established with the Roman and Chinese empires the Tocharians played a role in the rapid development of the trade routes. The treasure of Begram, the city to the north of Kaboul where the Tocharians' summer residence was located, gave an idea of the wealth and expanse of this trade: its decorated Roman plates of glass, its Indian furniture ornaments, its Alexandrine and Syrian windows, and its Chinese lacquer bowls are all objects which illustrate the luxuriousness of this cosmopolitan civilization.

The first Buddhist art in Pakistan, in the region of Gandhara, was in the 1st century AD. Contrary to the Indian tradition of the period, Buddha was given a human form and this would be taken up throughout the Buddhist world. If, however, it borrowed its realism and traditional draping from Indian art it also revealed, in the regular, oval faces and wavy hair, a Hellenistic contribution which triumphed in Hadda.

Fragment of small bottle, Dauphin, Afghanistan, Kapica region, Begram, 1st century, blown glass, 9.2 x 9.3 cm

Meditating Buddha, 1st-3rd century, Pakistan, Gandhara region, schist, H: 45 cm

Right page:
Standing Bodhisattva, detail, Pakistan, Gandhara region, Shahbaz-Garhi monastery, 1st-3rd century, schist, 120 x 42 cm

PAKISTAN AFGHANISTAN

These works are situated on the 1st floor

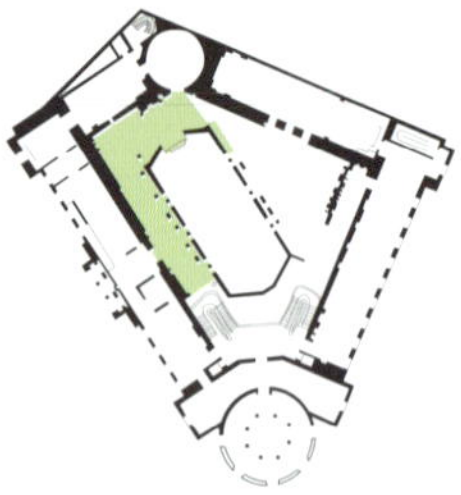

The art of Hadda

An important Buddhist monastic centre located in the south-east of Afghanistan, about twelve kilometres from the city of Jalalabad, and a famous pilgrimage place, Hadda produced a large quantity of vestiges of which there are almost fifteen thousand sculptures and more than five hundred *stupa*. The major works of the monasteries and the bas-reliefs were made of limestone, while the statutes were made of stucco. There were all painted and sometimes even decorated.

The oldest sculptures of Hadda were contemporaries with those of Gandhara. However, if the art which developed in Hadda from the 2nd century incontestably stemmed from the first Buddhist art, it clearly differentiates itself with a strong Hellenistic stamp from Hadda. This truly Greek enclave in the north of the country, set up as an independent kingdom upon the death of Alexander in 323 BC and the spread its culture in the plains of Jalalabad explained the transmission, not only of the iconographic themes but a sense of the visual arts coming from Greece. A companion of Buddha could just as well have the features of Hercules dressed in the lion of Neme's skin or those of Alexander the Great… The Greek tradition, thus serving Buddhism, produced a unique eclecticism in Hadda: certain figures, full of life and fantasy, clearly indicated an Hellenistic influence, delicate in the Greek-Roman draping, the crowns, the faces with tiny mouths and gentle smiles, while the others more directly evoked the radiant opulence of Indian art. Delicately modeled in stucco because of the rarity of stone, these sculptures displayed a remarkable liberty of expression accompanied by an admirable mastery of technique. This art disappeared in the 6th century and when the Chinese monk, Zuanzang, visited the site between 640 and 645 the monasteries were in ruin.

Spirit with flowers, Afghanistan, Hadda, 3rd-4th century, stucco, 72 x 24 cm

Head of young woman, Afghanistan, Hadda, Tapa-i-Kafariha monastery, 3rd-4th century, stucco, 16 x 13 cm

Head of Devata, Afghanistan, Hadda, 3rd-4th century, stucco, H: 13.5 cm

PAKISTAN AFGHANISTAN

These works are situated on the 1st floor

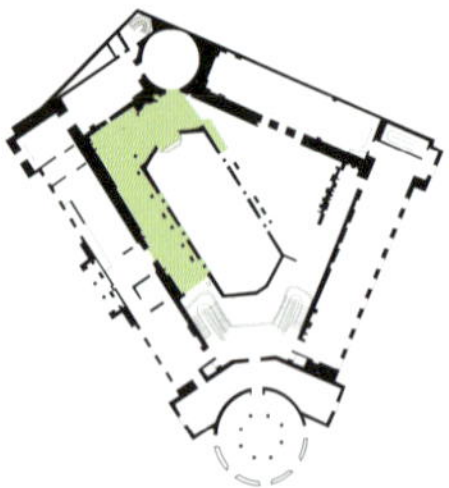

The end of Buddhist art: the monastery of Fondukistan

At the end of the 4th century, the Huns invaded Afghanistan. The regaining of the country by the Persian dynasty of the Sassanides restored a political and cultural stability which permitted Buddhist art to continue a while longer. On the road from China to India, in the fertile valley of Bamiyan where Buddhist monks were settled, monumental figures of Buddha were continued to be sculpted in the cliffs; the very ones the Taliban destroyed in the explosion in March, 2001. These figures influenced all of northern Asia.

The last works of Buddhist art were made in the monastery of Fondukistan, about one hundred and twenty kilometres from Bamiyan, in the 7th century. They were characterized by a mannered elegance. A *bodhisattva* was especially representative of this art: richly adorned, the long and slightly off-balanced torso, and the tilted head. It's rather heavy forms evoked India. As for the technique used, it is similar to the technique practiced in Central Asia where there was also a lack of stone: the sculptors modeled clay, added straw and horse's hair and then painted it.

Lodged in the monastery walls, these statuettes represented an important milestone between the art of Hadda and that of Kashmere, which prospered in the 8th and 9th centuries. As for Afghanistan, it passed into the hands of Moslems in the middle of the 7th century. Buddhist art then relinquished its place to Islamic art.

Buddha sitting in royal relaxation, Afghanistan, Ghorband valley, Fondukistan monastery, niche C, 7th century, clay 51 x 42 cm

Bodhisattva, detail, Afghanistan, Ghorband valley, Fondukistan monastery, niche D, 7th century, clay, 85 x 24 cm

NEPAL TIBET

These works are situated on the 1st floor

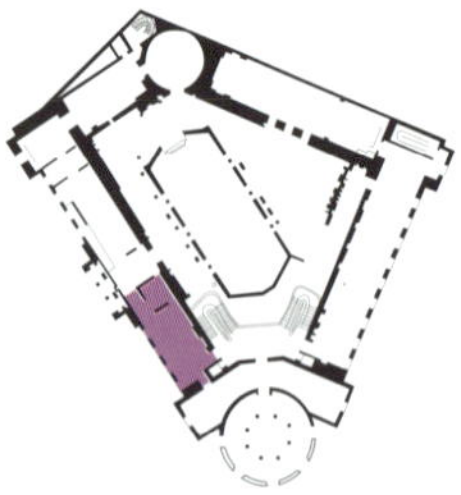

NEPAL

The valley of Katmandu originally made up all the Nepalese territory. Situated at an altitude of 1,500 metres and closed off in the north by the Himalaya mountains, it remained isolated from the great wave of exchanges in Asia for a long time. It was through India that this valley opened to exterior influences: the first dynasty attested to Nepal, in the 4th century AD, was connected to the Indian dynasty of the Gupta. Buddhism, already present in the valley, continued to spread. From the 8th century it's from India again that the inhabitants of Nepal, the Newars, borrowed from Tantric Buddhism. Founded on the *Tantra*, Sanskrit texts mixing philosophical speculations and practical magic, Tantric Buddhism developed remarkably in this region and inspired all artistic forms. A unique occurrence in the Indianized world, many works date from this period, according to a lunar era which began in 879. The oldest conserved paintings go back to the 11th century. They were paintings of illuminations and Buddhist and Hindu manuscript covers. On the Gandavyuha, if the elegant poses of the deities evoke Indian art, the choice and the arrangement of colours are characteristic of the Nepalese painting of the period. From 1200, under the Malla Dynasty, Nepal reached its political and economic peak. The sovereigns and a rich merchant aristocracy created many religious structures. At the same time the reputation of the Newars craftsmen, who excelled in making statuettes in bronze and gilded copper inlaid with precious stones, spread to China and Tibet.

In 1482 the valley was divided into three kingdoms whose capitals were Patan, Katmandu and Bhadgaon. During this period, called early Malla, the production of wooden statues and of great painted representations of Buddhist and Hindu divinities, like that of *Vajradhara*, the supreme Buddha and his deities, continued to develop.

In 1768 warriors descended from the Rajputs, the Gurkha, subjugated the three kingdoms and added new territories to them: modern Nepal was born.

Manjusri, bodhisattva of knowledge (?), Nepal, 13th century, gilded and inlaid copper, 50 x 20.3 cm

Manuscript cover of the Gandavyuha sutra, detail, Nepal, 12th century, gouache on wood, 6.6 x 57.4 cm

Vajradhara, the supreme Buddha and his divine servant, Nepal, 1488, gouache on canvas, 132 x 79.5 cm

NEPAL TIBET

These works are situated on the 1st floor

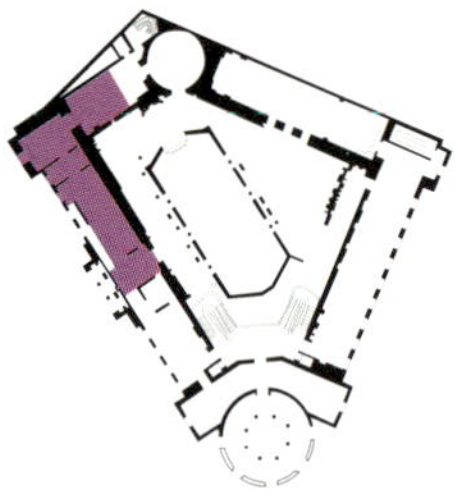

TIBET

The Fifth Dalai Lama (1617-1682) and its development

At the end of the 14th century, a reformer by the name of Tsong-kha-pa founded a new monastic order, that of the dGe-lugs-pa, the Virtuous. This order took on considerable importance from the end of the 16th century. In 1578 a pontiff, belonging paradoxically to another order, became the first *dalai* (which means "ocean of wisdom") and was recognized as the reincarnation of a disciple of the founder of the order of dGe-lugs-pa. With the coming of the Fifth Dalai Lama, the spiritual and worldly leader of the country and an exceptional politician but also a great administrator, builder and prolific writer, the order of the dGe-lugs-pa dominated Tibet. In one of the paintings representing him he appears wearing the yellow hat of the dGe-lugs-pa and is surrounded with insignias of his sacred character: the halo, the "thunderbolt-diamond", the bell and the prints of his hands and his feet. The "Great Fifth" is receiving the Mongol, Gu-shri Khan, represented under the seat of the pontiff. The meeting took place secretly in 1638 and its representation is part of the classical iconography of the Fifth Dalai Lama. Four years later Gu-shri Khan combated the three kings of oriental and central Tibet and offered the fruit of his victory to the Dalai Lama: a reunited Tibet, which had not been so since the fall of the empire in the 9th century.

Twenty-three years after the death of the Fifth Dalai Lama, in 1705, following a serious political crisis, the Chinese emperor Kangxi intervened in Tibet and the country progressively entered the orbit of its great neighbour. The goddess dPal-ldan-lha-mo, characteristic of the art after the reign of the Fifth Dalai Lama, illustrates the renewed Chinese influence. China too was influenced by Lamaism which, until 1911, would be one of the official religions of the country. Like the statue of the *bodhisattva* Manjusri, many Chinese works allude to Tibetan Buddhism.

The Fifth Dalai-Lama (1617-1682) receiving Gu-shri, the Khan of the Qoshot Mongols, Tibet, ca. 1700, tempera on canvas, 77 x 50 cm

Vajradhara, the supreme Buddha and his divine servant, Nepal, 1488, gouache on canvas, 132 x 79.5 cm

NEPAL TIBET

These works are situated on the 1st floor

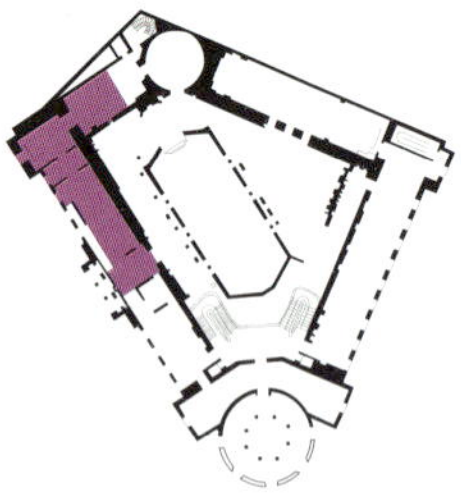

TIBET

The birth and formation of Tibetan art

Even more closed off than Nepal, Tibet is bordered by two massifs, the Himalayan mountains to the south and the Kunlun mountains to the north. Its average altitude of around 4,000 metres and its very hilly landscape frightened travellers at first, thus keeping it relatively isolated; certain trade routes would cross it however from the 4th century.

In the 7th century, King Songtsen Gampo started war with the China of the Tangs to conquer Central Asia. The foundation of the Tibetan Empire and the introduction to Buddhism in Tibet is attributed to him. Raised to the rank of official religion in the 8th century, Buddhism was suppressed in the following century when the Empire collapsed. One had to wait for the 11th century and the arrival in Tibet of a Buddhist master from Bengal, Atisha, in order for Tantric Buddhism to spread throughout the territory. The Tibetans in turn sent monks to be trained in India, namely in Kashmir and Bihar; many sculptures exhibit the influence of these two regions on the first art of Tibet.

In 1244 Tibet was conquered by Genghis Khan, the founder of the Mongol Empire. His grandson, who became the emperor of the China of the Yuan, designated monks from the Sa-skya monastery as viceroys of Tibet. From then on Tantric Buddhism played a major political role and the art which it inspired, supported by important Chinese imperial benefactors, developed considerably. As is illustrated in a stone sculpture representing Mahakala, the protector of the Buddhist doctrine, Tibetan art borrowed a great deal from Nepalese art. It was also influenced by the arts of China, Central Asia and India in the Pala period. It was this last movement that brought one closer to the painting representing Vajrasattva and figures around him, particularly because of the geometry of the faces and the treatment of the trees above the *bodhisattva* assistants.

Vajrasattva and his divine servant,
southern Tibet (?),
1st half of 13th century,
tempera on canvas, 59.6 x 51.3 cm

Mahakala, protector of the doctrine, in his manifestation as Gur-gyi mgon-po, Tibet, 1292, partially polychrome and gilded limestone, 47 x 28.5 cm

These works are situated on the 1st floor

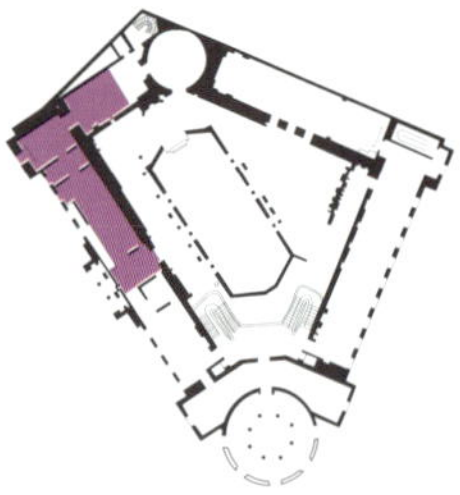

TIBET

The peak of Tibetan art

Even if Tibetan art displayed a great diversity owing to, in part, the geographical division of the land, from the 15th century it perfectly assimilated the different influences which contributed to its development and from then on displayed its own characteristics.

The works were used especially as supports for rituals and meditation and as their creations were assimilated into religious acts, the artists had to scrupulously respect the iconographic descriptions contained in the spiritual texts. Among the *thang-ka*, literally "something which unrolls", the *mandala*, composed of geometric figures, evoke the projection of the celestial palace of a god. These paintings, in the form of diagrams, are a perfect illustration of the close connection between the work of art and the liturgy. In the center of the *Mandala of Vajramrita*, the divine estate is protected by guards posted at the four doors. Surrounded by eight goddesses placed on the open petals of the lotus, the god is shown in the centre of the first circle with two principal objects of the Tibetan liturgy: the "the thunderbolt-diamond" or the *vajra*, which represents masculinity and the symbol of the path to Enlightenment, and the bell or *ghanta* which evokes femininity and the knowledge specific to Enlightenment.

Referred to under the name of Lamaism (from the term *lama*, which means "master"), Tantric Tibetan Buddhism developed so rapidly that all the institutions and social activities were strictly subjected to it. This theocracy reached its peak with the Fifth Dalai Lama.

Mandala of Vajramrita, Tibet, 1st half of 16th century, tempera on canvas, 83 x 72 cm

Two lamas from the order of Sa-skya-pa, detail, Tibet, 16th century, tempera on canvas, 64 x 52.8 cm

Titular God Samvara and his divine servant Vajravarahi, western Tibet (?), 16th-17th century, gilded brass, 35.8 x 21.5 cm

These works
are situated
on the 1st floor

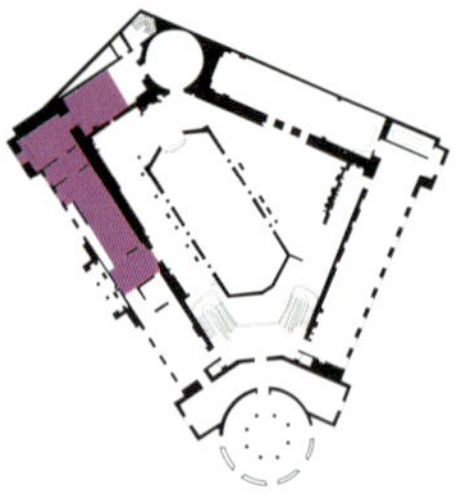

TIBET

The Fifth Dalai Lama (1617-1682) and its development

At the end of the 14th century, a reformer by the name of Tsong-kha-pa founded a new monastic order, that of the dGe-lugs-pa, the Virtuous. This order took on considerable importance from the end of the 16th century. In 1578 a pontiff, belonging paradoxically to another order, became the first *dalai* (which means "ocean of wisdom") and was recognized as the reincarnation of a disciple of the founder of the order of dGe-lugs-pa. With the coming of the Fifth Dalai Lama, the spiritual and worldly leader of the country and an exceptional politician but also a great administrator, builder and prolific writer, the order of the dGe-lugs-pa dominated Tibet. In one of the paintings representing him he appears wearing the yellow hat of the dGe-lugs-pa and is surrounded with insignias of his sacred character: the halo, the "thunderbolt-diamond", the bell and the prints of his hands and his feet. The "Great Fifth" is receiving the Mongol, Gu-shri Khan, represented under the seat of the pontiff. The meeting took place secretly in 1638 and its representation is part of the classical iconography of the Fifth Dalai Lama. Four years later Gu-shri Khan combated the three kings of oriental and central Tibet and offered the fruit of his victory to the Dalai Lama: a reunited Tibet, which had not been so since the fall of the empire in the 9th century.

Twenty-three years after the death of the Fifth Dalai Lama, in 1705, following a serious political crisis, the Chinese emperor Kangxi intervened in Tibet and the country progressively entered the orbit of its great neighbour. The goddess dPal-Idan-Iha-mo, characteristic of the art after the reign of the Fifth Dalai Lama, illustrates the renewed Chinese influence. China too was influenced by Lamaism which, until 1911, would be one of the official religions of the country. Like the statue of the *bodhisattva* Manjusri, many Chinese works allude to Tibetan Buddhism.

The Fifth Dalai-Lama (1617-1682) receiving Gu-shri, the Khan of the Qoshot Mongols, Tibet, ca. 1700, tempera on canvas, 77 x 50 cm

The goddess dPal-ldan-lha-mo, protector of the doctrine, in her manifestation as Kamadhatvisvari Parvati, Tibet, 1st half of 18th century, tempera on canvas, 130.5 x 107.5 cm

The First Panchen Lama (1569-1662), Tibet, late 17th-early 18th century, gilded copper, H: 31.3 cm

Manjusri, bodhisattva of wisdom, China, 18th century, partially polychrome gilded copper and brass, 15.5 x 10.5 cm

These works
are situated
on the 1st floor

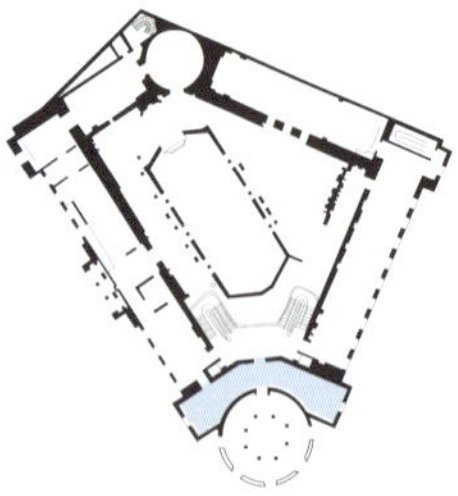

THE DECORATIVE ARTS OF INDIA: THE JEAN AND KRISHNA RIBOUD GALLERY

The Riboud Gallery displays the objects given to France by Jean and Krishna Riboud, who, until her death in 2000, was the president of the Association on Studying and documentation of Asian Textile. Textiles and costumes, arms, decorative objects and jewelry from the 16th to the 19th century evoke the splendor of the royal and princely courts of India and show the admirable technical skill achieved by the artists and craftsmen who worked for them. In comparison with the Rajputs kingdoms and the Sultanate of Deccan, Mughal India is particularly well-represented in the gallery. A sculpted panel in red sandstone, characteristic of Mughal architecture, evokes the carved niches in the palace where small bottles, vases, and fruit bowls, often in China, were kept, thus the name of chini khana, "porcelain house." The decorative arts also include arms to which the traditions of the country accord great importance and which are often genuine works of art. Thus the dagger handles carved in jade (called "victory stone") show very delicately carved animal settings: the heads of horses, rams, antelopes, camels, lions or falcons. From the middle of the 17th century they were inlaid with precious stones set in gold.

Textile art is also one of the most important industries of India of which Indian material has been renowned since antiquity. The major part of the production is made up of printed and painted cotton fabric, whose designs sometimes originate from Persia: arcatures, stylised foliage, trees of life… In the 18th century these fabrics made up an essential part of India's exports to Europe.

Architectural panel with niche decoration (chini khana),
Mughal India, ca. 1620, red sandstone, 85.5 x 96 cm

Bed linen, detail, northern India, Gujarat, late 18th-early 19th century, embroidered cotton, 44 x 228 cm

Dagger with horse-head handle, Mughal India, 18th century, jade, rubies and emeralds set in gold, tempered steel blade, L: 35.8 cm

Wine goblet, Mughal India, 18th century, jade, rubies and emeralds set in gold, H: 24 cm; D: 6 cm

Bird-shaped pendant, Mughal India (?), 18th century, gold, diamonds, rubies, emeralds, pearls and rock crystal, 10 x 6 cm

CHINA

These works are situated on the 2nd floor

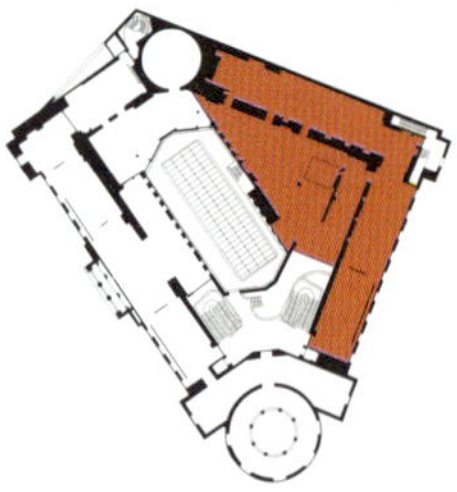

CLASSICAL CHINA

Calligraphy and painting

In China calligraphy goes beyond the art of well formed letters and is considered very important. Using simple means – a brush, ink, and paper or silk as a support – this subtle art requires an intense concentration on the part of the calligrapher and aims to reproduce, in the drawing of letters, the vital rhythm of the universe. This art began towards the end of the Han period (3rd century BC to 3rd century AD) and developed thanks to the erudite government who required a mastery of writing before granting access to power. It was an influence on all Chinese artistic expression and in particular, painting.

From the Tang period there appeared, beside portraits and animal representations where the preoccupation with resemblance was foreseen, landscape painting whose main aim was to evoke an atmosphere. It was however with the poet Wan Wei (699-759) that calligraphic painting truly first appeared: the monochrome ink wash drawing. The tools of the painter were abandoned for those of the calligrapher and landscape painting won its pre-eminence over figurative representations. Henceforth, put into the same category as writing, painting became the privilege of the intellectual elite.

Under the Five Dynasties in the 10th century and especially under the Northern Song (960-1279), calligraphic painting expressed the inner nature of the painter in front of a landscape, demonstrating thus a perfect mastery of the skill and a great spiritual quality. More lyrical under the Southern Song, at the end of the 12th and the beginning of the 13th century, landscape was refined under the Yuan (1280-1368), which was observable in the intimist art of Cao Zhibo. During the Ming period (1368-1644), Wen Zhengming and Liu Jue returned to models from the Yuan period. Under the Qing (1644-1911), in comparison with virtuoso art, a few independent artists stood out who, like Zhu Da, produced very plain works. It is remarkable that painting in China honours a tradition that has remained almost unchanged throughout its history and that no "revolution" stopped.

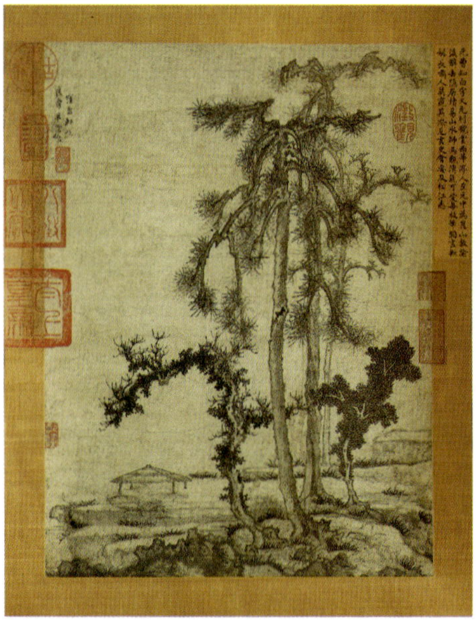

Cao Zhibo (1272-1360), *Villa under trees*, China, Yuan Dynasty, 1329, ink on paper, 162.5 x 66.5 cm

Wen Zhengming (1470-1553), *Voyage to the flat mountaintop*, China, Ming Dynasty, 1508, ink on paper, 49.5 x 29 cm

Zhu Da (1625-1705), *Trees and rocks*, China, Qing dynasty, 1694, ink on paper, 80 x 45 cm

CHINA

These works
are situated
on the 2nd floor

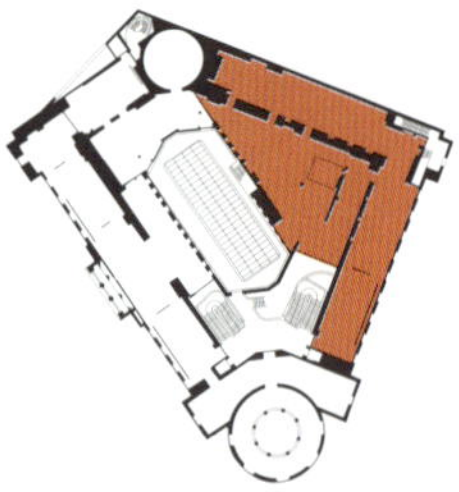

CLASSICAL CHINA

Ceramics under the Tang (618-907) and the Song (960-1279)

At the accession of the Tang, ceramic art had already had a long history: the first earthenware dates back to the Neolithic period; stoneware, baked at a temperature varying between 1,000 and 1,200 degrees and more solid than earthenware, dates back to the Zhou period (11th-3rd century BC); glazes which covered the pottery go back to the Han period (206 BC-220 AD); and lastly, the first white glazes appeared under the Sui (589-618). In the prosperous society of the Tang, who were very open to foreign influences, these methods underwent change. Inspired by Sassanide art, the glazes "three colors" appeared on plates with motifs of roses, birds, and clouds whose reliefs imitated pieces from Persian goldsmiths. The black ceramics with speckled motifs from Henan and the green stoneware with lotus and peony motifs from Zhejiang foreshadowed the celadon (gray-green glazed pottery) of the Song period. The major invention of the period however was the making, in Northern China in the 9th century, of pieces baked at a very high temperature: porcelain. Ceramics reached an admirable classicism with the refined culture of the Song. From the colours used in the Tang period followed monochromes in subtle tones and thick glazes on which the pattern appeared discreetely. The celadon of Longquan especially marked the height of the green stoneware technique. The forms were equally refined and their sinuous profiles, limited often to a continuous, curved line ending up in a tiny opening contributed to the harmony of the whole.

Flat tripod decorated with flowers and birds, China, Tang Dynasty, 8th century, sandstone, decoration incised on slip, H: 7.6 cm; D: 31 cm

Pitcher with double spouts in the shape of phoenix heads, northern China, Shaanxi, Yaozhou, late 5 Dynasties period-early northern Song Dynasty, 2nd half of the 10th century, gray sandstone covered with celadon, cut and engraved decoration, H: 20.5 cm

Vase, northern China, Jin Dynasty, 12th-13th century, gray sandstone with white slip, decoration in iron-brown under transparent glaze, 42.5 x 20 cm

CHINA

These works are situated on the 2nd floor

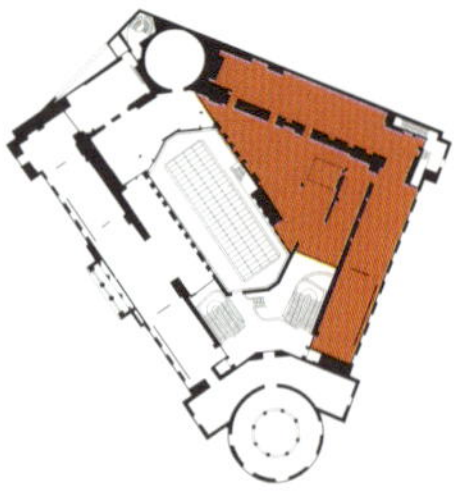

CLASSICAL CHINA

The Mongol influence: the Liao (907-1125) and the Yuan (1280-1368)

While the Song were governing almost all of China, a Mongol empire developed in the 10th century in the northeast of China and in Manchuria. In 986 it took the name of the Liao empire and ended up, in the 11th century, encroaching on the provinces in the north of China. The Liao, of nomadic origin, gradually settled due to contact with Chinese civilization. A new court handcraft appeared which borrowed advanced techniques from the Chinese while favouring forms which came from the culture of the steppes and affirmed a pronounced taste for colour. Thus very singular objects appeared: ceramics evoking the form of the goatskin bag used by the nomad people but covered with polychrome engravings such as those done by the Tang, and masks and crowns in chiseled silver… The Liao Empire collapsed in 1125 under the battles of a newcomer, but it prefigured the Mongol Empire which conquered China over a century later.
Born of a federation of people from the steppes, the Mongol Empire of the Yuan brought profound disruption to China. The cultivated society disappeared and the country multiplied its exchanges with foreign countries. It was the period of the voyages of Marco Polo, the diffusion of Chinese inventions such as printing or gun powder, of the settlement in China of the first Moslem communities and the propagation of Tibetan Lamaism.
Ceramics benefited from the rapid development of commercial exchanges: thus the cobalt imported from Persia by China at the beginning of the 14th century permitted the creation of new ceramics, the "blue and white", where the patterns took on greater importance. From the workshops of Longquan for the celadon and from Jingdezhen for the "blue and white" came monumental pieces mainly intended for the princely courts of India and western Asia.

Gourd, northern China, Liao Dynasty, 10th-12th century, terracotta with glaze on slip, H: 27.4 cm

Funerary mask, northern China, Liao Dynasty, 10th-12th century, embossed silver, H: 22 cm

Right page: *Meiping vase*, southern China, Jiangxi, Jingdezhen, Yuan Dynasty, mid 14th century, porcelain with dragon motif on cobalt blue background under glaze, H: 35 cm

CHINA

These works are situated on the 2nd floor

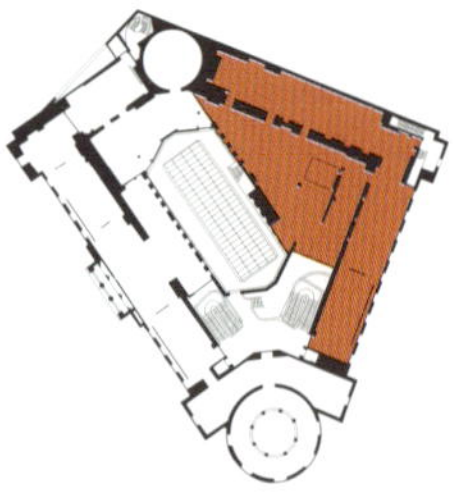

CLASSICAL CHINA

The blossoming of the arts under the Ming (1368-1644)

The uprisings against the Mongol occupants ended in 1368 in the founding of the Ming Empire by the head of a revolt. An immense programme of reconstruction got underway, aimed at restoring the cities and the roads as well as restablishing a brilliant civilization. In 1409 the Emperor Yongle thus gathered 2,169 learned men to write an enormous encyclopedia containing 100,970 chapters. In 1420 the rebuilt Peking was raised to the rank of imperial capital.

At the time there was an unprecedented development of porcelain and it represented the main part of the ceramic production. Located not far from the coast, in the south-east of the country, the ancient factory of Jingdezhen became the most important in the country; it exported a large part of its production by sea – mainly the "blue and white" – which it adapted to the tastes of different countries. The size of this business was revealed by whole cargoes of Chinese porcelain found in the wreckage of Dutch and Portugese ships which, from the middle of the 15th century, disputed the control of the maritime routes in the Pacific.

The coming of the Ming Dynasty also marked the return of scholars to the social and cultural life of the country. In the domain of ceramic they showed a preference for the monochromes, and in furniture they restored honour to traditional cabinetmaking which, in addition to ceremonial furniture in lacquer reserved for the court, produced very sober, hard wood furniture. In 1567 the lifting of the ban on importing exotic wood gave a real impetus to the art of furniture which then reached its peak. Sculpted in dense wood, tulip-wood, rosewood..., the *Ming* furniture is characterized by the remarkable technique of mortice and tenon joint.

Cabinet and armchairs with horseshoe-shaped back, China, Ming Dynasty, early 17th century, rosewood (huanghuali), cabinet, H: 127 cm

Gourd with floral decoration: branch and camellia, China, Jiangxi, Jingdezhen, Ming Dynasty, early Yongle period (1403-1424), porcelain, 24.9 x 21.4 cm

Bowl with dragon-shaped handles, China, Ming Dynasty, 16th century, white jade, translucent, veined, sculpted, engraved, H: 4.9 cm

KOREA

These works are situated on the 2nd floor

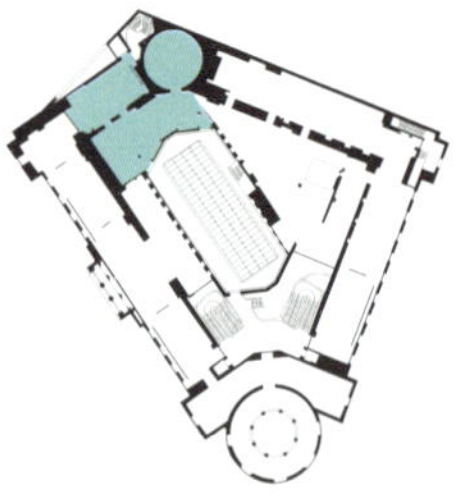

The birth of the kingdom of Korea

Situated at the eastern extremity of the Asian continent and endowed with long maritime shorelines, Korea found itself at the cross-roads of several civilizations. From the horsemen of the steppe it borrowed, between the 8th and 7th centuries BC, the use of the horse and the technique of bronze. From China it owes the use of iron and during the occupation of the north of the peninsula by the Han, from 108 BC to 313 AD, writing and the introduction to Buddhism. If it was influenced by China, Korean Buddhist art, which developed from the 4th century, distinguished itself by its discreet refinement and stamp of reserve, as is seen in the little statuette of *Bodhisattva meditating*.

Politically, from the 1st century, the Korean territory was organized around three kingdoms: Paekche in the south-west, Koguryo in the north and Silla in the south-east. From this last kingdom, as its distance preserved it from the Chinese assaults by the Souei and the Tang, came a bronze crown found in a royal tomb which reveals the influence of the art of the steppes, notably from Siberian art, on the culture of the Silla.

This kingdom would be moreover the last to convert to Buddhism during the 6th century. In 668 it allied with the Tang and conquered the kingdom of Paekche as well as a part of the kingdom of Koguryo. Henceforth Korea was practically unified and Chinese influence was seen everywhere. However the fall of the Tang in 906 prompted a new kingdom.

In 918 the country was taken over by the Koryo dynasty. Firstly influenced by China, the sculpture contained large figures of Buddha with soft forms and traits of a great serenity. As for ceramics, which was largely dominated by the celadon, it developed considerably and differentiated itself from the Song models by a greater naturalism and the inlay of floral motifs. The utmost quality which characterized it was such that it was extolled in a Chinese work in 1125.

Bodhisattva meditating, Korea, Paekche Kingdom, Three Kingdoms period, 6th century, gilded bronze, 15 x 5 cm

Bottle, Korea, Koryo period, 12th-13th century, celadon, inlaid decoration under glaze, 32,5 x 19,4 cm

Right page: *Crown*, Korea, Silla Kingdom, Three Kingdoms period, 5th-6th century, gilded bronze, 30 x 17 cm

KOREA

These works are situated on the 2nd floor

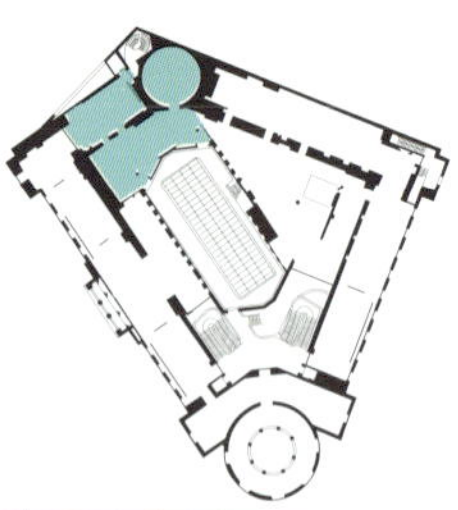

The influence of Korea (1392-1592)

In 1392, after the Mongols' devastation of Korea, the country found peace again with the Choson monarchy. Though it recognized the suzerainty of the China of the Ming and adopted Confucianism as the official religion, the new dynasty in power nevertheless asserted its singularity: it founded its new capital in Seoul and gave the country a specific, complete alphabet.

Going back to the dawn of this new period, three stone sculptures which represent sitting monks revealed traits of Korean art that were found later on in the painting: naturalism but also imagination and humour. Many works of this type were found in Korea. Like the two stone sculptures, each of these figures presents a facial characteristic, naturally ironic features, of which in the diversity and audacity never cease to amaze.

As for ceramics, it developed once again, aided by the prosperity of the country. The art of celadon was followed with the ceramic *Punch'ong*, which owes its name to its powdered green color. If, in the beginning, it went back to the inlay work of the Koryo period, this art subsequently evolved toward abstract patterns painted in black.

At the same time, white porcelain, newly imported from China, was intended for the court; its austerity conformed to the Confucian ideal that was highly valued by the aristocracy. It was produced in royal workshops and at times presented motifs which were similar to calligraphy.

In 1592 and in 1598, in rapid succession, two Japanese invasions caused the ruin of Korea. They were finally driven out with the support of the Ming but the wars drained the country. Many ovens were destroyed; the ceramic *Punch'ong* ceramics disappeared in the 16th century.

Bottle, Korea, Choson period, 15th-16th century, Punch'ong ceramics, incised and champleve decoration under glaze; H: 24 cm

Three sitting monks, Korea, Choson period, 14th-15th century, stone, 33 x 24 cm, 31 x 32 cm, 30 x 25 cm

KOREA

These works
are situated
on the 2nd floor

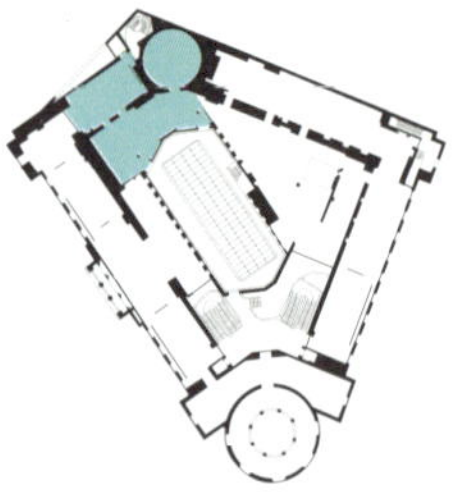

The hermit kingdom

After a new invasion, this time led by the Mandchous in 1635, the kingdom of Korea had to accept the suzerainty of its conquerors. It withdrew into itself, called itself the "hermit kingdom", and developed a classical art which borrowed a great deal from the Ming dynasty. One had to wait until the 18th century for the arts to recover a vigour and inventiveness typically Korean. The renaissance took place in painting. At first very influenced by China, Korean painting progressively freed itself from these models by borrowing its subjects from the country itself, whether a landscape or a war scene. With the painter Chong Son (1676-1759) there appeared thus the first Korean landscapes painted from life. These are of small groups painted in pastoral settings under cherry trees in bloom or of horses in nature. It is in the war scenes however that Korean art excelled and found its verve and its humour once again, namely in the works of one of the greatest masters of the period, Kim Hong-do (1745-1814). Whether it is travellers meeting each other on the road or even the arrival of a notable in his sedan chair, the artist makes the whole Choson society live again with a remarkable delicacy. The same human diversity characterized the Korean masks used during village festivals, where it was amusing to caricature the contemporary society. Even the religious banners which accompanied the revival of Buddhism echoed this regained confidence: on the banner of the *Amrta Raja*, which evokes hope in the Paradise of the West, the different classes of the Korean court and clergy were captured with as much precision as humour.

Mask, the shaman, Korea, Choson period, 18th century, wood, touches of paint and cloth, 24 x 19 cm

Yi Han-ch'ol, *Ten- panel folding screen: flowers and birds*, detail, Korea, Choso period, 19th century, colours on silk, 197 x 420 cm

Ambrosia painting or Amrta Raja, Korea, Kyonggi-do, Kukch'ong-sa Temple, Choson period, 1755, colours on silk, 159 x 196 cm

Kim Hong-do, *Eight-panel folding screen: genre scenes*, detail, Korea, Choson period, 18th century, ink and colours on silk, H: 80.4 cm

JAPAN

These works
are situated
on the 2nd floor

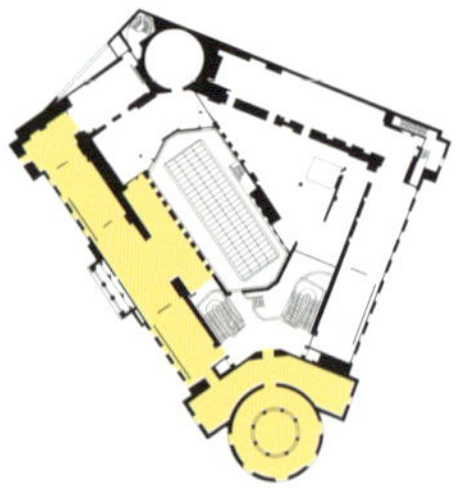

From the dawn of the civilization to the formation of the Japanese state

Made up of some twenty thousand islands, of which there are four principal islands, the Japanese archipelago was settled by successive waves of people coming from Siberia, the South Pacific, China and Korea. The first ceramic appeared around 10500 BC. Characterised by rope-cord patterns on clay, called *jomon*, it gave its name to the period in which, for almost ten milleniums, it developed. As well as useful objects, found also are pots with exuberant shapes, often asymmetrical, whose frequently pointed bottoms rendered them rather unusable, and also there were anthropomorphic clay figurines, *dogu*, called "snow goggles" because their eyes are often surrounded with a circle. In all likelihood, at first linked to a fertility cult, the use of the *dogu* grew more diversified: the fact that a certain number of these figurines were voluntarily broken seems to indicate a propitiatory rite, whereas the perforation of certain others suggests that they could have been used as reliquaries.
Towards 400 BC, this original art disappeared suddenly and the culture which came after it, called the Yayoi, made ceramics without any decoration. In contact with China of the Han and the Wei, this civilization is characterized by their use of bronze and iron. It seems to have known a lot of infighting, attested to by the defensive structures of the villages, equipped with watch-towers and moats.
From the 3rd century AD the idea of a national unity appeared while Japanese soil was covered with great tombs built in the form of earthen mounds characterized by their "key-hole" shape, *kofun*, which gave its name to the period. *Haniwa* (clay cylinders) are clay figurines in the round representing men, animals, houses or symbolic objects whose meaning isn't clear, which were placed atop or around the kofun. In the 6th century the introduction of Buddhism into Japanese society put an end to these burial customs and to the art which served them.

Figurine dogu "snow goggles",
Japan, late Jomon period,
1000-300 BC,
terracotta, H: 22 cm

Right page:
Haniwa: Warrior, Japan,
late Kofun period, 6th century,
baked clay, H: 112 cm

JAPAN

These works are situated on the 2nd floor

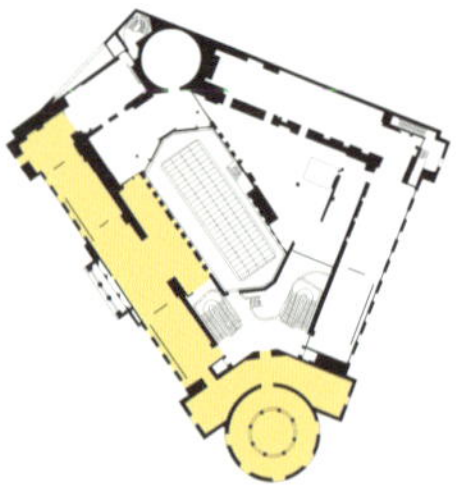

The introduction of Buddhism

In 552, Song-Myong, the Korean king of Paekche, seeking to create an alliance with Japan, sent to the Japanese emperor several Buddhist presents accompanied by an essay which praised this religion: "This law is the most excellent of all laws, difficult to understand and difficult to fathom [...] That's why [...] we are sending our minister, in order that he passes it on to your empire and propagates it inside the country." In spite of the resistance of the conservative clan of Motonobe who were attached to the cult of native divinities, the *Kami*, Buddhism was adopted by the Japanese state before the end of the 6th century. From 624 the Annals of Japan mentioned forty-six monasteries in the territory. Benefiting from contributions of Korean artists, Japanese Buddhist art developed rapidly. It resolutely took up a place in the wake of Chinese art; likewise, the new capital, Nara, was founded on the model of the Chang'an of the Tang.

Soon the Buddhist monasteries had gained such strong political influence that it worried the authorities: the beginning of the Heian period, from 794, thus marked a clear slowing down of artistic activity connected to Buddhism. Far from the aristocratic realism of the Nara period, the art of this period, in giving a more personal interpretation of the great Buddhist figures, freed itself progressively from the Chinese influence. The political difficulties the Tang had then culminated in the Japanese emancipation: in 894 the country temporarily ended its relations with China. Under the Fujiwara (894-1185), a powerful, aristocratic family, and then with the warrier clan Kamakura (1185-1333), led by generals, the shogun, new forms of devotion appeared: Zen Buddhism and the Schools of the Pure Land. They extolled faith in Amida, the Buddha of everlasting light, of whom artists made monumental representations.

Bosatsu (bodhisattva), Japan, Nara period (710-794), dry lacquer, traces of azure blue in the hair, 59.5 x 20.2 cm

Amida-nyorai, the buddha Amitabha forming the gesture of preaching, Japan, 2nd part of the Heian period, Fujiwara period, 11th-12th century, wood, H: 84 cm

Right page: *Portrait of priest Jishin Osho (1230-1316), from the Ritsu sect of the Sadaiji Temple in Nara*, detail, Japan, Kamakura period (1185-1336), 1st half of the 14th century, painting on silk, H: 130 cm

JAPAN

These works are situated on the 2nd floor

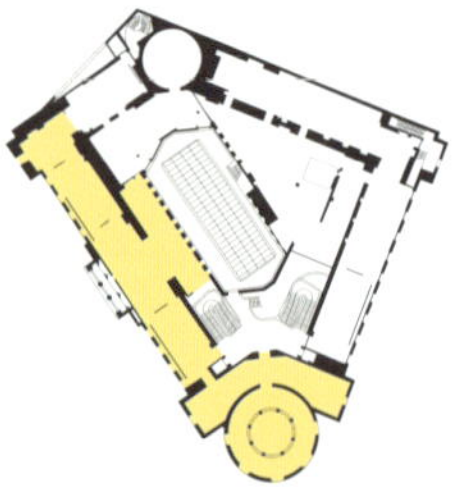

The development of the Japanese culture

At the end of the 13th century, the invasion of China by the Mongols pushed many Chinese monks to emigrate to Japan. There they spread a philosophy founded on meditation, *Chan* in Chinese, *Zen* in Japanese. Very quickly this doctrine, which stressed self-confidence and spiritual self-discipline, conquered the new class of warriors in power.

Raku tea bowl, attributed to Koetsu, Japan, Kyoto, Momoyama period, 1558-1637, terracotta, H: 7.8 cm; D: 14.5 cm

The first *Zen* temple in Japan was founded on a Chinese Song model in 1253 in Kamakura, the capital at the time. It was especially though in professing moderation, simplicity, and spontaneity, that Zen culture gave birth to a new art of living which brought about a real blossoming of the so-called minor arts. Inside houses with very little furniture or mainly low furniture, folding screens and long paintings called *kakemono*, one drank tea in accordance with codified rituals of the tea ceremony. Outside rock gardens were cultivated and in entertainment places, there was a theatre of complex forms, the Noh, chanted drama and dance where the actors wear masks. Thus there developed around the Zen art of living a whole formal language, subtle and austere, supported by an urban culture in expansion based on the power of the merchants. This multiform art flourished during the period of the Momoyama dictatorship between 1573 and 1603. At the end of the period it had achieved its highest expression in ceramics, *Raku*, in which simplicity, combined with subtle irregularities embodied the *Zen* ideal. The Japanese culture had henceforth found its mode of expression.

In 1543, the landing of the Portuguese in the archipelago marked the first encounter of the Japanese with the West. It gave rise to an exotic fashion which the folding screens of "Barbarians from the South" illustrate: with their oversized costumes topped with undersized heads, the foreigners here are represented in a resolutely humouristic manner.

Portrait of man, Japan, early Edo period, early 17th century, wood with traces of lacquer and colours, eyes inlaid with rock crystal, 56 x 52 cm

Folding screen of Namban Byobu called "the Portuguese", detail, Japan, Edo period, Kano school, 17th century, colours on paper, 170 x 380 cm

JAPAN

These works
are situated
on the 2nd floor

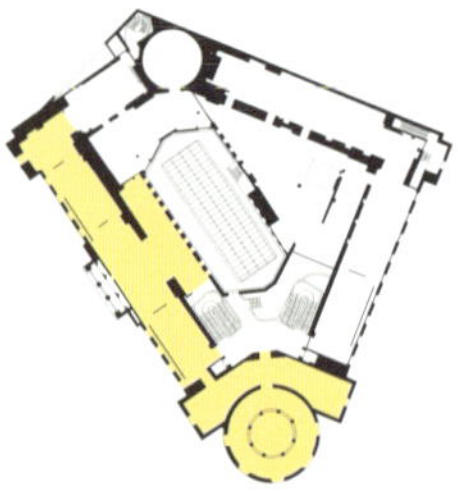

The Edo period and the "images of the floating world"

In 1603 a new *shogun*, Tokugawa Ieyasu, took power in Japan. He subdued the *daimyo*, the military chiefs of the region, and their *samurai* and founded the village of Edo, the future name for Tokyo, the administrative and military capital of the country. Kyoto remained however the city where the emperor resided and the artistic reference. It is also here that painting developed and evolved first of all, particularly the war scenes. On the folding screens that in times past were mainly decorative, painters now represented characters close-up. The artists of Edo were inspired firstly by the art of Kyoto. Very quickly however they transformed it, adapting it to the tastes of their clients. While Kyoto lost its hegemony, Edo developed considerably until it became, at the beginning of the 18th century, a capital of a little over one million inhabitants. On imposing on the feudal chiefs the responsibility of seeing to the upkeep of rich residences and staying with their troups regularly, the *shogun* maintained a population fond of entertainment in the city. The pleasure quarters developed and inspired paintings of many scenes of this genre. The polychrome print assured a large diffusion and little cost for these new subjects that were called *ukiyo-e*, "images of the floating world". In the materialistic society of Edo, the term was understood as an incitement to take advantage of the pleasures of this world and depict them in images. If Utamaro essentially painted portraits of women, Hokusai and Hiroshige showed a partiality for the landscape. Their works attest to the discovery of the Western perspective, introduced in Japan with the works which came from Europe in Dutch ships, the only ones admitted at that time, with Chinese boats, into the port of Nagasaki.

Utamaro Kitagawa (1753-1806), *The Courtesan Hanaogi from the Ogiya tea house, Snow, moon, flower* series, print, 36.2 x 24.9 cm

Hiroshige Utagawa (1797-1858), *The Great Bridge: sudden shower in Atake*, from *One hundred famous places of Edo*, 1856-1858, print, 45.4 x 75.7 cm

Hokusai Katsushika (1760-1849), *Under the wave at Kanagawa*, series of *Thirty-six views of Mount Fuji*, print, 25.5 x 38.2 cm

These works
are situated
on the 3rd floor

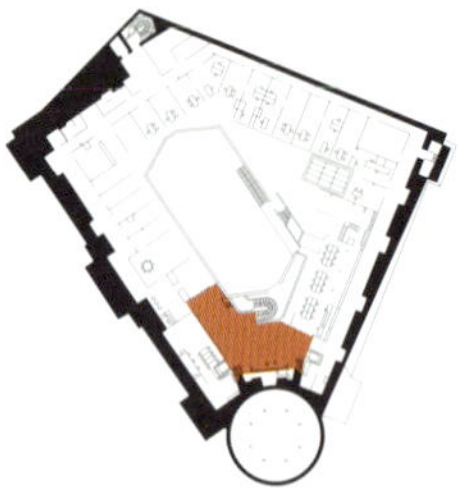

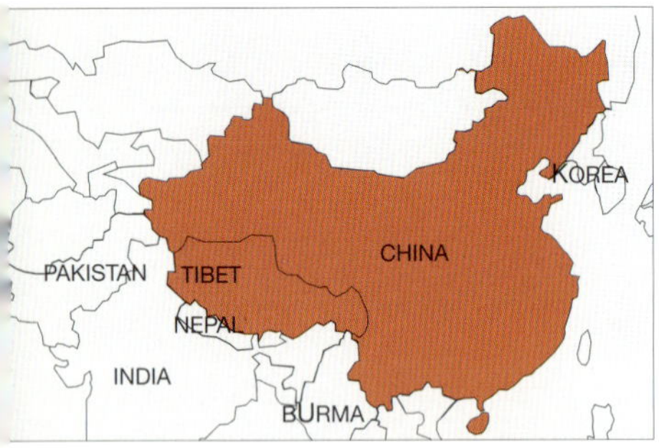

CLASSICAL CHINA

The influence of the imperial workshops: the Qing Dynasty (1644-1911)

Before dealing with the catastrophic economic situation and the revolts that it had brought about, the Ming first of all thought that they had found a potential ally in the Mandchous. In fact, the Mandchous turned out to be the new invaders and the Chinese could not stop the capture of Peking and then the foundation of the Mandchoue dynasty of the Qing in 1644. The first years of the occupation were extremely hard, but with the arrival of the Emperor Kangxi, in 1662, a change occurred; the emperor sought to win over the Chinese intellectual elite in furthering the arts through important patronage. The Jingdezhen factory was reorganized and, in 1680, an imperial workshop was set up in Peking. The art of enamel, which had begun to develop under the Ming, continued with the Qing to develop remarkably and exhibited a great mastery in the use of colours: thus, towards 1720, in the Peking workshops, a pink enamel (famille-rose palette) was perfected, competing with the "green family" palette which was then in vogue. From 1728 the introduction of new colours once again multiplied the possibilities offered by this art. The most frequently used procedure was the cloisonné: coloured molten glass applied decoratively on the ceramic is delimited by fine bands of metal which melt during the baking. Real technical feats were accomplished as is seen in the *Vase with "a thousand flowers"*. Under the reign of Qianlong (1736-1795) the production reached its peak with monumental pieces of over two metres in height.
With the successive reigns of Kangxi, Yougzheng and Qianlong, between 1662 and 1795, China experienced more than one century of stability and in 1774 the country had more than two million inhabitants. It extended its authority over Nepal, Burma, Siam, Vietnam and Korea and maintained a vast network of diplomatic and commercial relations with foreign countries, up to the court of Louis XIV.

Vase with "a thousand flowers", southern China, Jiangxi, Jingdezhen, Qing Dynasty, late Qianlong period (1736-1795), porcelain decorated with polychrome enamels from the "Famille rose", H: 48 cm; D: 36 cm

Plate with floral decoration, southern China, Jiangxi, Jingdezhen, Qing Dynasty, Yongzheng period (1723-1735), white porcelain decorated with polychrome enamels from the "Famille rose", D: 20.9 cm

CHINA

This work is situated on the 3rd floor in the Lacquer Rotunda

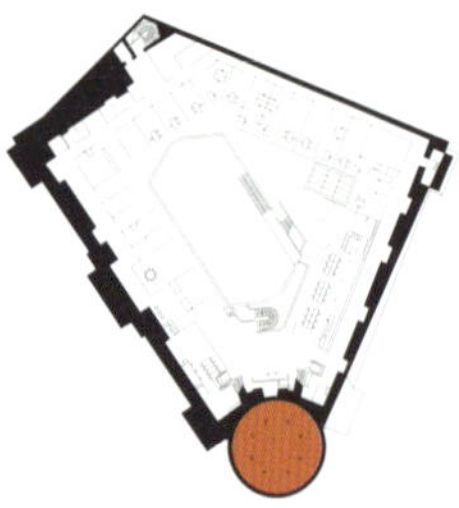

The Lacquer Rotunda

Lacquer is the sap of a tree originating in China, the *Rhus verniciflua*; it is obtained by incising the trunk before being filtered and heated. Its colour is more often black or red and it can also be mixed with gold or silver powder. Applied in successive coats, most often on wood, it can then be sculpted or inlayed with precious materials. The first evidence of this art of lacquer in China dates back to the Neolithic period. Because of the highly skilled technique necessary in the making of objects in lacquer, this material has always been reserved for objects de luxe. Under the Ming and the Qing, it was intended exclusively for ceremonial furniture which often embellished the palace of the emperor and the court lords.
It is the case for folding screens called "of Coromandel", the name of the Indian coast from where the first expeditions left for Europe. Very sought after in Europe in the 17th and 18th centuries, in France these folding screens aroused an intense enthusiasm in cabinet makers who, in turn, applied their talents to this new material.

Twelve-panel folding screen decorated with thrushes, pine trees and clouds, China, Qing Dynasty, 1712, Kangxi period, lacquered wood, "Coromandel" lacquer, 320 x 624 cm

BUDDHIST PANTHEON

Hotel Heidelbach
19, avenue d'Iena
75016 Paris

Buddhist Pantheon Galleries

The Buddhist Pantheon Galleries, installed in 1991 in a mansion formerly belonging to Alfred Heidelbach, just a few steps away from the Guimet Museum, at 19 Avenue d'Iena, display some 250 Japanese Buddhist works and some 30 Chinese works which cast light on all aspects of the Japanese Buddhist pantheon and the Chinese and Indian influences entwined in its history. Following the different representations of Buddha, there appeared the great Enlightened Ones or *bodhisattva*, the "Kings of Science" or *vidyaraja*, the divinities and finally the patriarchs, distinguished monks and other spiritual teachers of Buddhism. These collections thus revived the founding project of Emile Guimet, who dedicated the museum of his dreams to "the history of human thought" through the great religions of the world, as well as through aesthetic contemplation. In 2001 a traditional tea house was built in the Japanese garden of the Buddhist Pantheon Galleries; tea ceremonies are organized there, to which the public is invited to attend upon reservation.

Mosuke Yamamoto (19th century), replica of the *Mandala of Kobo Daishi from the Kod of the Toji temple* (23 pieces), lacquered and gilded wood

View of the Tea Pavillion, Japanese garden of the Buddhist Pantheon galleries

crédits photographiques

RMN/Arnaudet : p. 20, 34, 37, 38, 39, 42, 43, 44, 48, 49, 52, 55, 71, 75 ; RMN/Asselberghs R. : p. 30 ; RMN/Bellot M. : p. 49 ; RMN/Berizzi J.-G. : p. 51 ; RMN/Blot G. : p. 46 ; RMN/Bréjat H. : p. 72 ; RMN/Costa Evandro : p. 45 ; RMN/Dubois N. : p. 31, 56, 61, 62, 63, 64, 65 ; RMN/Goldings J. : p. 18 ; RMN/Lambert R. : p. 25, 26, 27, 28, 29, 36, 40, 54, 57, 59, 67, 70, 73, 74 ; RMN/Lewandowski H. : p. 8, 9, 10, 11, 12, 13 ; RMN/L'Hoir J. : p. 68, 76, 77 ; RMN/Ollivier T. : cover, p. 6, 7, 14, 15, 16, 18, 19, 21, 22, 24, 25, 26, 28, 35, 36, 41, 46, 50, 51, 55, 56, 59, 60, 64, 65, 66, 68, 70, 72, 78, 79 ; RMN/Ollivier T./Urtado M. : p. 17 ; RMN/Pleynet P. : p. 20, 60 ; RMN/Ravaux : p. 32, 33, 47, 49, 78 ; RMN : p. 23, 53, 58, 69 ; RMN/Urtado M. : p. 14, 18, 33

achevé d'imprimer
le 20 janvier 2004
sur les presses d'Aramis à Rennes
dépôt légal février 2004